The Little Book of Simple Quilting

The Little Book of Simple Quilting

NEW
HOLLAND

First published 2013 by
New Holland Publishers Pty Ltd
London • Sydney • Cape Town • Auckland

Garfield House 86–88 Edgware Road London W2 2EA United Kingdom
Wembley Square First Floor Solan Road Gardens Cape Town 8001 South Africa
1/66 Gibbes Street Chatswood NSW 2067 Australia
218 Lake Road Northcote Auckland New Zealand

www.newhollandpublishers.com

Copyright © 2013 New Holland Publishers
Copyright © 2013 in text New Holland Publishers
Copyright © 2013 in images: New Holland Publishers
Quilt design © 2013 Sally Ablett, Sharon Chambers, Katharine Guerrier, Marion Patterson, Mary O'Riordan,
Susan A Warren, Rita Whitehorn, Alison Wood

All rights reserved. No part of this publication may be reproduced, stored in a retrieval system or transmitted, in any form or by any means,
electronic, mechanical, photocopying, recording or otherwise, without the prior written permission of the publishers and copyright holders.

A record of this book is held at the British Library and the National Library of Australia

ISBN 978 1 78009 4 465

Managing Director: Fiona Schultz
Publisher: Lliane Clarke
Designer: Lorena Susak
Illustrators Carrie Hill and Coral Mula
Photographs: Mark Winwood and Shona Wood
Production director: Olga Dementiev
Printer: Toppan Leefung Printing Ltd (China)

10 9 8 7 6 5 4 3 2 1

Keep up with New Holland Publishers on Facebook http://www.facebook.com/NewHollandPublishers

Contents

Introduction 7

The Basics 9

Materials 10

Equipment 12

Techniques 15

The Quilts 30

Portugal Strippy 32

Water's Edge 36

Fan Quilt 42

Quillow 48

Diamond Quilt 54

Twinkling Star 60

Squares and Stars 67

Hidden Stars 75

Row of Flowers 83

Sister's Choice 88

Spider's Web 94

Jacob's Ladder 100

Blue-and-white Ohio Stars Bed Quilt 106

Summer Fields 116

Floral Garland Quilt 122

Index 128

Introduction

Patchwork has evolved from a skill of necessity to a craft of popular pleasure today. Where once women would have cut up old clothes and faded household fabrics with the intention of eking out scarce and expensive resources, today's quilters have thousands of fabrics in every design and hue at their ready disposal, all sold in convenient quantities ready for cutting and piecing into patchwork quilts.

Yet, the tradition of the quilters of yesteryear lives on in the designs that are made today. With limited means the quilters of the past sought to create objects of great beauty, as well as practical and cherished furnishings for their homes. They would have amassed their fabrics over many years and as a result would incorporate cloth into their designs that had specific memory associations. Women carefully pieced together their quilts, laboriously folding each patch of fabric over a paper template and hand stitching the patches together. They followed intricate patterns and created delightful cloths that showcased their ingenuity and skill. Geometric designs using squares, triangles and strips made economical and convenient use of the fabric. A quilt top may take years to complete and be the culmination of meticulous planning. No wonder then, that they were held in such high regard.

In their designs, each quilter sought to balance the tonal values of their cloths creating optical illusions and exciting visual effects with areas of light and shade fashioned by the careful placement of each fabric choice. Once patched together, the paper templates would be removed and a quilt 'sandwich' incorporating the patchwork cloth, a layer of insulation such as an old blanket, and a backing fabric would be put together. At this stage the completion of the quilt may have become a communal one, with women forming 'quilting bees' to stitch the three layers together.

The quilting stage offers another opportunity to add depth and design to the quilt surface. A quilting pattern can follow the lines of the patchwork pieces, picking out shapes and designs and creating areas of relief on the quilt surface, or it can introduce an entirely new design. The quilting stitch may be a running stitch neatly and evenly worked. Alternatively, areas of the quilt can be tied together with threads or stitched together at specific points and decorated with buttons.

This beautiful book showcases 15 fabulous traditional patchwork quilt designs. Together they demonstrate how beautiful fabrics can create attractive and appealing effects that can be used to enhance the style and décor of a room. Sewing machines make light work of the once time-consuming task of patching a quilt top together. Contemporary techniques that make use of rotary cutting equipment and ingenious labour-saving 'chain-piecing' methods make cutting and stitching patchwork pieces together simpler and more accurate. Each of these techniques is described in detail in the introduction. Included too is a description of the essential tools and material that you will need to begin.

Several of the quilts are small in scale, making them ideal projects for a novice or someone with little time to spare. Water's Edge, for instance, makes use of a pack of colour-coordinated fabrics sold as a 'layer cake', which conveniently takes the thinking out of choosing fabric and is a good choice for someone unsure of picking a successful colourscheme. These large patches are simply cut to size and pieced together in a simple design. Similarly, Spider's Web makes use of small amounts of bold and bright fabrics, which are stitched at random to fill a background block. The large blocks are then stitched together to form the whole.

For quilters with more time to spare, there are quilts made using four-patch through to sixteen-patch blocks, traditional harlequin, Jacob's ladder, and there's even an appliqué fan quilt design. Each is illustrated with step-by-step illustrations and easy-to-follow instructions so that you can make a fabulous quilt that you can be proud of.

The Basics

Materials

PATCHWORK FABRICS

The easiest fabrics to work with for patchwork are closely woven, 100 per cent cotton. They "cling" together making a stable unit for cutting and stitching, they don't fray too readily and they press well. Quilting shops and suppliers stock a fantastic range in both solid colours and prints, usually in 115 cm/45 in widths, and most of the quilts in this book are based on these cottons.

BACKING AND BINDING FABRICS

The backing and binding fabrics should be the same type and weight as the fabrics used in the patchwork top. They can be a co-ordinating colour or a strong contrast. You could also be adventurous and piece the backing, too, to make a reversible quilt. In either case, the colour of the binding needs to work with both the top and the backing fabric designs.

WADDING (BATTING)

Various types of wadding (batting) are available in cotton, polyester, wool or mixed fibres. They can be bought in pre-cut sizes suitable for cot quilts and different sizes of bed quilts or in specific lengths cut from a bolt. They are also available in different weights or "lofts" depending on how padded you want the quilt to be. Lightweight polyester wadding is the most commonly used, but some wool or cotton types are more suited to hand quilting. Some need to be closely quilted to prevent them from bunching up; others can be quilted up to 20 cm/8 in apart. Follow the manufacturer's instructions if in doubt.

QUANTITIES

The quantities given at the beginning of each project have been calculated to allow for a bit extra – just in case! A few of the quilts combine cutting down the length of the fabric with cutting across the width. This is to make the most economical use of fabric or to obtain border pieces cut in one piece.

Unless otherwise stated, any 25.5 cm/10 in requirement is the "long" quarter – the full width of the fabric – and not the "fat" quarter, which is a piece 50 x 56 cm/ 18 x 22 in.

PREPARATION

All fabrics should be washed prior to use in order to wash out any excess dye and to avoid fabrics shrinking at different rates. Wash each fabric separately and rinse – repeatedly if necessary – until the water is clear of any colour run. If washing in a machine, cut a piece of white fabric from a larger piece. Place one piece in with the wash. After the wash, compare the white fabric with its other half. If they are the same, the fabric did not run. If a particular fabric continues to colour the water no matter how many times it is washed/rinsed and you have your heart set on using it, try washing it together with a small piece of each of the fabrics you intend to use with it. If these fabrics retain their original colours, i.e. they match the pieces not washed with the offending fabric, you would probably be safe in using it. But if in doubt – don't! Once washed and before they are completely dry, iron the fabrics and fold them selvage to selvage – as they were originally on the bolt – in preparation for cutting. Be sure to fold them straight so that the selvages line up evenly, even if the cut edges are not parallel (this will be fixed later).

THREADS

For machine quilting use lightweight or monofilament threads. For quilting by hand, use a thread labelled "quilting thread", which is heavier than normal sewing thread. Some threads are 100 per cent cotton; others have a polyester core that is wrapped with cotton. You can use a thread either to match or to contrast with the fabric that is being quilted.

Alternatively, use a variegated thread toning or contrasting with the patchwork. It is also acceptable to use several colours on the same piece of work. If the quilt is to be tied rather than quilted, use a heavier thread, such as coton perlé, coton à broder or stranded embroidery cotton.

Equipment

There are some essential pieces of equipment that have revolutionized the making of patchwork quilts. Rotary cutting equipment, consisting of a rotary cutter used with an acrylic ruler and self-healing cutting mat, has speeded up the process of cutting shapes and made it more accurate; the sewing machine makes assembling the patchwork and quilting the finished piece quick and easy.

SEWING MACHINES

Evermore sophisticated, computerized machines are now available, but even a machine with just a straight stitch will speed up the process of assembling and quilting the patchwork considerably. Most sewing machines have a swing needle that allows the zig-zag stitching used for securing appliqué patches. Machines with decorative stitches provide the opportunity for additional embellishments.

LONG-ARM QUILTING MACHINES

These machines are used by professional quilters who have a huge library of quilting designs at their disposal. There is also the option to have edge-to-edge quilting, all-over quilting of one design over the entire quilt, or a combination of patterns to complement each other. Alternatively, you can specify your own free-hand style.

One of the advantages of this machine is that the quilt sandwich does not need to be tacked or pinned together prior to quilting: the pieced top, wadding (batting) and backing are mounted onto separate rollers that are part of the frame of the machine. The machine is hand operated and takes considerable skill to work successfully. Most of the quilters who offer this quilting service advertize in patchwork magazines.

ROTARY CUTTING

Rotary cutting has become the most commonly used method of cutting fabrics for patchwork. Most rotary cutting tools are available with either imperial or metric measurements.

Rotary cutters There are several different makes available, mainly in three different sizes: small, medium and large. The medium size (45 mm/1¾ in) is probably the one most widely used and perhaps the easiest to control. The smallest can be difficult to use with rulers. The largest is very useful when cutting through several layers of fabric but can take some practice to use. The rotary blade is extremely sharp, so always observe the safety instructions. It does become blunted with frequent use, so be sure to have replacement blades available.

Rotary rulers Various different rulers are available for use with rotary cutters. These are made of acrylic and are sufficiently thick to act as a guide for the rotary blade. You must use these rulers with the rotary cutter. Do not use metal rulers, as they will severely damage the blades.

The rulers are marked with measurements and angled lines used as a guide when cutting the fabrics. Ideally, these markings should be on the underside of the ruler, laser printed and easy to read. Angles should be marked in both directions. Different makes of rulers can have the lines printed in different colours. Choose one that you find easy on your eyes. Some makes also have a non-slip surface on the back – a very helpful addition. The two most useful basic rulers are either a 60 x 15 cm/ 24 x 6 in, or one that is slightly shorter, and the small bias square ruler, 15 cm/6 in. This ruler is particularly useful for marking squares containing two triangles – the half-square-triangle units. There are many other rulers designed for specific jobs that you can purchase if and when needed.

Self-healing rotary cutting mats These are essential companions to the rotary cutter and ruler. Do not attempt to cut on any other surface. The mats come in a number of different sizes and several different colours. The smaller ones are useful to take to classes, but for use at home, purchase the largest that you can afford and that suits your own work-station. There is usually a grid on one side, although both sides can be used. The lines on the mat are not always accurate, so it's better to use the lines on the ruler if possible.

OTHER USEFUL EQUIPMENT

Most other pieces of equipment are those that you will already have in your workbox. Those listed below are essential, but there is also a vast array of special tools devised by experienced quiltmakers that have specific uses. They are not needed by the beginner quilter but can really enhance the planning, cutting and quilting of your designs.

Scissors Two pairs are needed. One large pair of good-quality scissors should be used exclusively for cutting fabric. The second, smaller pair is for cutting paper, card (card stock) or template plastic.

Markers Quilting designs can either be traced or drawn on the fabric prior to the layering or added after the layering with the aid of stencils or templates. Various marking tools are available: 2H pencils; silver, yellow or white pencils; fade away or washable marking pens; and Hera markers (which lightly indent the fabric). Whatever your choice, test the markers on a scrap of the fabric used in the quilt to ensure that the marks can be removed.

Pins Good-quality, clean, rustproof, straight pins are essential when a pin is required to hold the work in place for piecing. Flat-headed flower pins are useful because they don't add bulk.

Safety pins These are useful for holding the quilt "sandwich" together for quilting, especially for those who prefer to machine quilt or want the speed of not tacking/basting the three layers together. Place the pins at regular intervals all over the surface.

Needles For hand quilting, use "quilting" or "betweens" needles. Most quilters start with a no. 8 or 9 and progress to a no. 10 or 12. For machine stitching, the needles numbered 70/10 or 80/12 are both suitable for piecing and quilting. For tying with thicker thread, use a crewel or embroidery needle.

Thimbles Two thimbles will be required for hand quilting. One thimble is worn on the hand pushing the needle and the other on the hand underneath the quilt "receiving" the needle. There are various types on the market ranging from metal to plastic to leather sheaths for the finger. There are also little patches that stick to the finger to protect it.

Hoops and frames These are only needed if you are quilting by hand. They hold a section of the quilt under light tension to help you to achieve an even stitch. There are many types and sizes available, ranging from round and oval hoops to standing frames made of plastic pipes and wooden fixed frames. Hoops are perhaps the easiest for a beginner. The 35 cm/ 14 in or 40 cm/16 in are best for portability. Many quilters continue to use hoops in preference to standing frames. When the quilt is in the hoop, the surface of the quilt should not be taut, as with embroidery. If you place the quilt top with its hoop on a table, you should be able to push the fabric in the centre of the hoop with your finger and touch the table beneath. Without this "give", you will not be able to "rock" the needle for the quilting stitch. Do not leave the quilt in a hoop when you are not working on it, as the hoop will distort the fabrics.

Techniques

ROTARY CUTTING

The basis of rotary cutting is that fabric is cut first in strips – usually across the width of the fabric, then cross-cut into squares or rectangles.

MAKING THE EDGE STRAIGHT

Before any accurate cutting can be done, first make sure the cut edge of the fabric is at right angles to the selvages.

1 Place the folded fabric on the cutting mat with the fabric smoothed out, the selvages exactly aligned at the top and the bulk of the fabric on the side that is not your cutting hand. Place the ruler on the fabric next to the cut edge, aligning the horizontal lines on the ruler with the fold and with the selvages.

2 Place your non-cutting hand on the ruler to hold it straight and apply pressure. Keep the hand holding the ruler in line with the cutting hand. Place the cutter on the mat just below the fabric and up against the ruler. Start cutting by running the cutter upwards and next to the edge of the ruler (diagram 1).

DIAGRAM 1

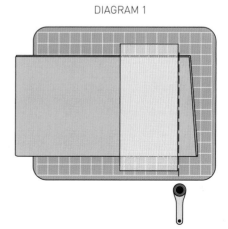

3 When the cutter becomes level with your extended fingertips, stop cutting but leave the cutter in position and carefully move the hand holding the ruler further along the ruler to keep the applied pressure in the area where the cutting is taking place. Continue cutting and moving the steadying hand until you have cut completely across the fabric. Close the safety shield on the cutter. If you run out of cutting mat, you will need to reposition the fabric, though this is not ideal.

4 Open out the narrow strip of fabric just cut off. Check to make sure that a "valley" or a "hill" has not appeared at the point of the fold on the edge just cut; it should be perfectly straight. If it is not, fold the fabric again, making sure that this time the selvages are exactly aligned. Make another cut to straighten the edge and check again.

CUTTING STRIPS

The next stage is to cut strips across the width of the fabric. To do this, change the position of the fabric to the opposite side of the board, then use the measurements on the ruler to cut the strips.

1 Place the fabric on the cutting mat on the side of your cutting hand. Place the ruler on the mat so that it overlaps the fabric. Align the cut edge of the fabric with the vertical line on the ruler that corresponds to the measurement that you

wish to cut. The horizontal lines on the ruler should be aligned with the folded edge and the selvage of the fabric.

2 As before, place one hand on the ruler to apply pressure while cutting the fabric with the other hand (diagram 2).

DIAGRAM 2

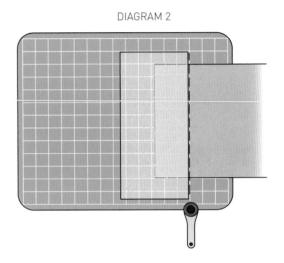

CROSS-CUTTING

The strips can now be cut into smaller units, described as cross-cutting, and these units are sometimes sub-cut into triangles.

Squares

1 Place the strip just cut on the cutting mat with the longest edge horizontal to you and most of the fabric on the side of the non-cutting hand. Cut off the selvages in the same way in which you straightened the fabric edge at the start of the process.

2 Now place the strip on the opposite side of the mat and cut across (cross-cut) the strip using the same measurement on the rule as used for cutting the strip; ensure that the horizontal lines of the ruler align with the horizontal edge of the fabric. You have now created two squares of the required measurement (diagram 3). Repeat as required.

DIAGRAM 3

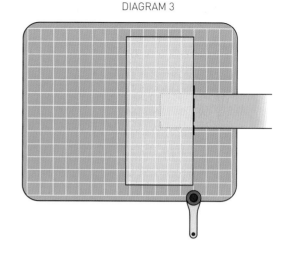

Rectangles

1 First cut a strip to one of the required side measurements for the rectangle. Remove the selvages.

2 Turn the strip to the horizontal position as for the squares.

3 Cross-cut this strip using the other side measurement required for the rectangle. Again, ensure that the horizontal lines of the ruler align with the horizontal cut edges of the strip.

Wide strips

Placing two rulers side by side can aid the cutting of extra-wide strips. If you don't have two rulers, place the fabric on the cutting mat in the correct position for cutting. Align the cut edge of the fabric with one of the vertical lines running completely across the cutting board, and the folded edge with one of the horizontal lines. If the measurement does not fall on one of the lines on the cutting mat, use the ruler in conjunction with the cutting mat.

Multi-strip units

This two-stage method of cutting strips, then cross-cutting into squares or rectangles, can also be used to speed up the cutting of multi-strip units to provide strip blocks.

1 Cut the required number and size of strips and stitch together as per the instructions for the block/quilt you are making. Press the seams and check that they are smooth on the right side of the strip unit with no pleats or wrinkles.

2 Place the unit right side up in the horizontal position on the cutting mat. Align the horizontal lines on the ruler with the longer cut edges of the strips and with the seam lines just created (diagram 4). If, after you have cut a few cross-cuts, the lines on the ruler do not line up with the cut edges

as well as the seam lines, re-cut the end to straighten it before cutting any more units.

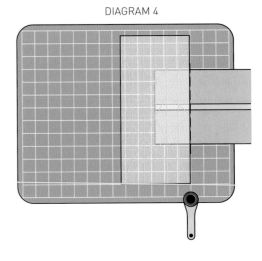

DIAGRAM 4

ROTARY CUTTING TRIANGLES

Squares can be divided into either two or four triangles, called half-square or quarter-square triangles. Both sizes of triangle can be quickly cut using the rotary cutter or they can be made even faster by a quick piecing method described on the following pages.

Cutting half-square triangles

1 Cut the fabric into strips of the correct depth and remove the selvages. Cross-cut the strips into squares of the correct width.

2 Align the 45° angle line on the ruler with the sides of the square and place the edge of the ruler so that it goes diagonally across the square from corner to corner. Cut the square on this diagonal, creating two half-square triangles (diagram 5).

zontal lines of the ruler with the long edge of the triangle, the 45° line with the short edge of the triangle and the edge of the ruler placed on the point of the triangle opposite the long edge. Cut this half-square triangle into two quarter-square triangles.

DIAGRAM 5

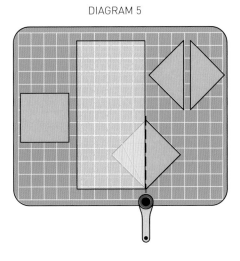

DIAGRAM 6

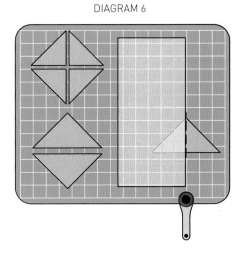

Cutting quarter-square triangles

1 Cut the fabric into strips of the correct depth and remove the selvages.

2 Cross-cut the strips into squares of the correct width. Cut the square into two half-square triangles, as before.

3 You can either repeat this procedure on the other diagonal (diagram 6) or, if you are wary of the fabric slipping now that it is in two pieces, separate the two triangles and cut them individually. Align one of the hori-

SEAMS

To stitch accurately, you must be able to use the correct seam allowance without having to mark it on the fabric. To do this, you use the foot or the bed of your sewing machine as a guide. Many machines today have a "7.5 mm/¼ in" or "patchwork" foot available as an extra. There are also various generic foot accessories available that will fit most machines. Before you start any piecing, check that you can make this seam allowance accurately.

Checking the machine for the correct seam allowance

Unthread the machine. Place a piece of paper under the presser foot, so that the right-hand edge of the paper aligns with the right-hand edge of the presser foot. Stitch a seam line on the paper. A row of holes will appear. Remove the paper from the machine and measure the distance from the holes to the edge of the paper. If it is not the correct width, i.e. 7.5 mm/¼ in, try one of the following:

1 If your machine has a number of different needle positions, try moving the needle in the direction required to make the seam allowance accurate and stitch a row again.

2 Draw a line on the paper to the correct seam allowance, i.e. 7.5 mm/¼ in from the edge of the paper. Place the paper under the presser foot, aligning the drawn line with the needle. Lower the presser foot to hold the paper securely and, to double-check, lower the needle to ensure that it is directly on top of the drawn line.

3 Fix a piece of masking tape on the bed of the machine so that the left-hand edge of the tape lines up with the right-hand edge of the paper. This can also be done with magnetic strips available on the market to be used as seam guides. But do take advice on using these if your machine is computerized or electronic.

Stitching 7.5 mm/¼ in seams

When stitching pieces together, line up the edge of the fabric with the right-hand edge of the presser foot or with the left-hand edge of the tape or the magnetic strip on the bed of your machine, if you have used this method.

Checking the fabric for the correct seam allowance

As so much of the success of a patchwork depends on accuracy of cutting and seaming, it is worth double-checking on the fabric that you are stitching a 7.5 mm/¼ in seam.

Cut three strips of fabric 4 cm/1½ in wide. Stitch these together along the long edges. Press the seams away from the centre strip. Measure the centre strip. It should be exactly 2.5 cm/1 in wide. If not, reposition the needle/tape and try again.

Stitch length

The stitch length used is normally 5 to the centimetre or 12 stitches to the inch. If the pieces being stitched together are to be cross-cut into smaller units, it is advisable to slightly shorten the stitch, which will mean the seam is less likely to unravel. It is also good practice to start each new project with a new needle in a clean machine – free of fluff around the bobbin housing.

QUICK MACHINE PIECING

The three most basic techniques are for stitching pairs of patches together (chain piecing), for stitching half-square triangle units and for stitching quarter-square triangle units.

Chain piecing

Have all the pairs of patches or strips together ready in a pile. Place the first two patches or strips in the machine, right sides together, and stitch them together. Just before reaching the end, stop stitching and pick up the next two patches or strips. Place them on the bed of the machine, so that they just touch the patches under the needle. Stitch off one set and onto the next. Repeat this process until all the pairs are stitched to create a "chain" of pieced patches/strips (diagram 7). Cut the thread between each unit to separate them. Open out and press the seams according to the instructions given with each project.

DIAGRAM 7

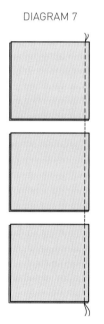

Stitching half-square triangle units

This is a quick method of creating a bi-coloured square without cutting the triangles first.

1 Cut two squares of different coloured fabrics to the correct measurement, i.e. the finished size of the bi-coloured square plus 1.75 cm/⅝ in. Place them right sides together, aligning all raw edges. On the wrong side of the top square, draw a diagonal line from one corner to the other.

2 Stitch 7.5 mm/¼ in away on each side of the drawn line (diagram 8).

DIAGRAM 8

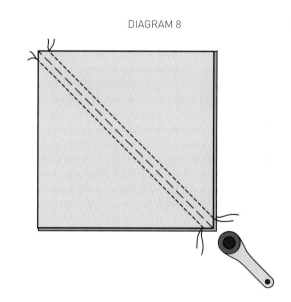

3 Cut the two halves apart by cutting on the drawn line. Open out and press the seams according to the instructions given with each project. You now have two squares, each containing two triangles. Trim off the corners (diagram 9).

DIAGRAM 9

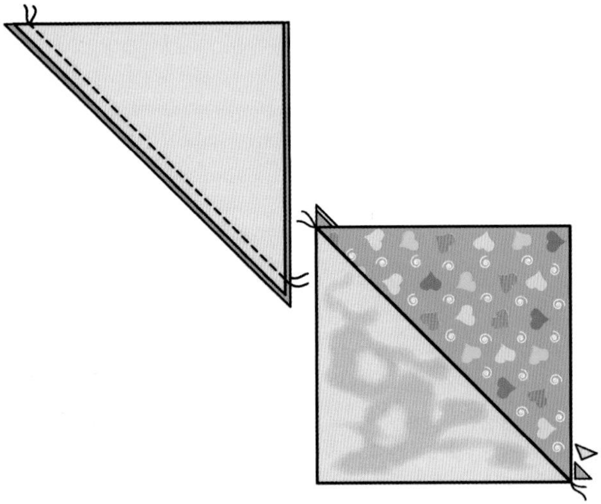

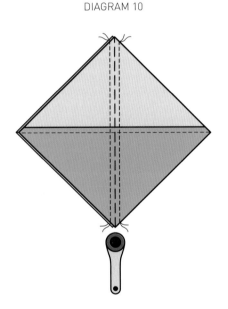

Stitching quarter-square triangle units

This method also creates triangles from squares without first cutting the triangles.

1 Cut squares to the finished size of a square containing four triangles plus 3.5 cm/1¼ in. Follow the stitching, cutting apart and pressing sequence as for the half-square triangles units.

2 Place the two bi-coloured squares right sides together. Ensure that each triangle is facing a triangle of a different colour. Draw a line diagonally from corner to corner, at right angles to the stitched seam.

3 Pin carefully to match the seams, then stitch 7.5 mm/¼ in away on each side of the line. Before cutting apart, open up each side and check to see that the points match in the centre (diagram 10).

DIAGRAM 10

4 Cut apart on the drawn line. You now have two squares, each containing four triangles (diagram 11).

DIAGRAM 11

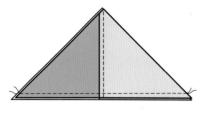

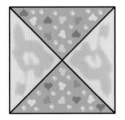

PRESSING

Each project will have instructions on the direction in which to press the seam allowances. These have been designed to facilitate easier piecing at junctions and to reduce the bulk so that seam allowances do not lay one on top of the other. Pressing as you complete each stage of the piecing will also improve the accuracy and look of your work. Take care not to distort the patches. Be gentle, not fierce, with the iron.

ADDING THE BORDERS

Most patchwork tops are framed by one or more borders. The simplest way of adding borders is to add strips first to the top and bottom of the quilt and then to the sides, producing abutted corners. A more complicated method is to add strips to adjacent sides and join them with seams at 45 degrees, giving mitred borders. Only the first method is used for the quilts in this book.

Adding borders with abutted corners

The measurements for the borders required for each quilt will be given in the instructions. However, it is always wise to measure your own work to determine the actual measurement.

1 Measure the quilt through the centre across the width edge to edge. Cut the strips for the top and bottom borders to this length by the width specified for the border.

2 Pin the strips to the quilt by pinning first at each end, then in the middle, then evenly spaced along the edge. By pinning in this manner, it is possible to ensure that the quilt "fits" the border. Stitch the border strips into position on the top and bottom edge of the quilt (diagram 12). Press the seams towards the border.

DIAGRAM 12

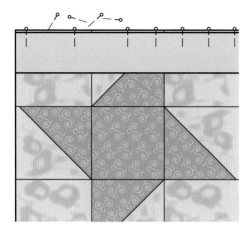

3 Measure the quilt through the centre from top to bottom. Cut the side border strips to this measurement.

4 Pin and stitch the borders to each side of the quilt as before (diagram 13). Press the seams towards the border.

DIAGRAM 13

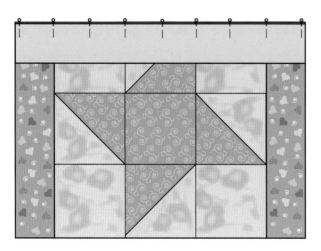

QUILTING

The three layers or "sandwich" of the backing/wadding/pieced top are held together by quilting or by tying. The quilting can be done by hand or machine. The tying is done by hand stitching decorative ties at strategic points on the quilt. Buttons can also be used.

Layering/sandwiching

Prior to any quilting, unless you are using a longarm quilting machine, the pieced top must be layered with the wadding and the backing. The wadding and the backing should be slightly larger than the quilt top – approximately 5 cm/2 in on all sides. There are two different methods for assembling the three layers depending on whether the quilt has bound edges or not.

Assembling prior to binding

1 Arrange the backing fabric wrong side uppermost. Ensure that it is stretched out and smooth. Secure the edges with masking tape at intervals along the edges to help to hold it in position.

2 Place the wadding on top of the backing fabric. If you need to join two pieces of wadding first, butt the edges and stitch together by hand using a herringbone stitch (diagram 14).

DIAGRAM 14

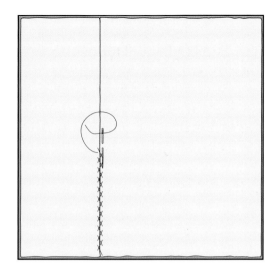

3 Place the pieced top right side up and centred on top of the wadding.

Assembling where no binding is used ("bagging out")

1 Spread out the wadding on a flat surface. Smooth out to ensure there are no wrinkles.

2 Place the backing fabric centrally on top of the wadding, right side uppermost.

3 Place the pieced top centrally over the backing, wrong side uppermost. Pin with straight pins around the edges to keep them together.

4 Stitch around all four sides with a 7.5 mm/¼ in seam allowance but leaving an opening of about 15–18 in/35–45 cm in one of the sides.

5 Trim the excess wadding and backing at the sides and across the corners to reduce bulk, then turn the quilt right side out, so that the wadding is in the middle. Slip-stitch the opening closed.

6 Smooth out the layers of the quilt and roll and fingerpress the edges so that the seam lies along the edge or just underneath.

Basting prior to quilting

If the piece is to be quilted rather than tied, the three layers now need to be held together at regular intervals. This can be done by basting or by using safety pins. For either method, start in the centre of the quilt and work out to the edges.

Using a long length of thread, start basting in the centre of the quilt top. Only pull about half of the thread through as you start stitching. Once you have reached the edge, go back and thread the other end of the thread and baste to the opposite edge. Repeat this process, stitching in a grid of horizontal and vertical lines over the whole quilt top (diagram 15).

DIAGRAM 15

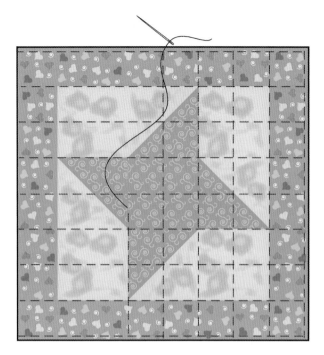

MACHINE QUILTING

Designs to be used for machine quilting should ideally be those that have one continuous line. The lines can be straight or free-form curves and squiggles. For either type, be sure to keep the density of stitching the same. With either method, continuous lines of stitching will be visible both on the top and on the back of the quilt. It is a quick method but requires careful preparation.

There is a wide variety of tools available designed to help make handling the quilt

easier during the machine quilting process. Practice is essential.

It is worth making up a practice sandwich – if possible using the same fabrics and wadding as used in the actual quilt – to be sure that you get the effect you want. In any case, plan the quilting design first, otherwise there is a danger that you will start with quite dense stitching, then tire of the process and begin to space out the lines, producing an uneven pattern.

When starting and stopping the stitching during machine quilting, either reduce the stitch length to zero or stitch several stitches in one spot. If you don't like the build-up of stitches that this method produces, leave long tails on the thread when you start and stop. Later, pull these threads through to one side of the quilt, knot them, then thread them into a needle. Push the needle into the fabric and into the wadding, but not through to the other side of the quilt, and then back out through the fabric again about 2.5 cm/1 in away from where the needle entered the quilt. Cut off the excess thread.

In-the-ditch machine quilting

One of the easiest and most common forms of straight line quilting is called "in-the-ditch" and involves stitching just beside a seam line on the side without the seam allowances. Some machines require a walking foot to stitch the three layers together. These are used with the feed dogs up and, while in use, the machine controls the direction and stitch length.

Free-motion machine quilting

When machine quilting in free-hand, a darning foot is used with the feed dogs down, so that you can move the quilt forwards, backwards and sideways. This is easier on some machines than others, but all require a bit of practice.

HAND QUILTING

The stitch used for hand quilting is a running stitch. The needle goes into the quilt through to the back and returns to the top of the quilt all in one movement. The aim is to have the size of the stitches and spaces between them the same.

1 Thread a needle with an 45 cm/18 in length of quilting thread and knot the end. Push the needle into the fabric and into the wadding, but not through to the back, about 2.5 cm/1 in away from where you want to start stitching. Bring the needle up through the fabric at the point where you will begin stitching. Gently pull on the thread to "pop" the knot through into the wadding.

2 To make a perfect quilting stitch, the needle needs to enter the fabric perpendicular to the quilt top. Holding

the needle between your first finger and thumb, push the needle into the fabric until it hits the thimble on the finger of the hand underneath.

3 The needle can now be held between the thimble on your sewing hand and the thimble on the finger underneath. Release your thumb and first finger hold on the needle. Place your thumb on the quilt top just in front of where the needle will come back up to the top and gently press down on the quilt (diagram 16).

DIAGRAM 16

4 At the same time, rock the thread end of the needle down toward the quilt top and push the needle up from underneath so that the point appears on the top of the quilt. You can either pull the needle through now, making only one stitch, or rock the needle up to the vertical again, push the needle through to the back, then rock the needle up to the quilt top, again placing another stitch on the needle. Repeat until you can no longer rock the needle into a completely upright position (diagram 17). Pull the needle through the quilt. One stitch at a time or several placed on the needle at once – "the rocking stitch" – before pulling the thread through, are both acceptable.

5 When the stitching is complete, tie a knot in the thread close to the quilt surface. Push the needle into the quilt top and the wadding next to the knot, but not through to the back of the quilt. Bring the needle up again about 2.5 cm/1 in away and gently tug on the thread to "pop" the knot through the fabric and into the wadding. Cut the thread.

DIAGRAM 17

BINDING

DIAGRAM 18

Once the quilting is completed, the quilt is usually (but not always) finished off with a binding to enclose the raw edges. This binding can be cut on the straight or on the bias. Either way, the binding is usually best done with a double fold. It can be applied in four separate pieces to each of the four sides, or the binding strips can be joined together and stitched to the quilt in one continuous strip with mitred corners. To join straight-cut pieces for a continuous strip, use straight seams; to join bias-cut pieces, use diagonal seams (diagram 18).

For either method, the width of the bias strips should be cut to the following measurement: (finished binding width x four) + (the seam allowance x two).

For example, a finished binding width of ½ in would be cut as 2½ in:

(½ in x 4) + (¼ in x 2) = 2½ in

or 1.25 cm would be cut 6.5 cm:

(1.25 cm x 4) + (7.5 mm x 2) = 6.5 cm

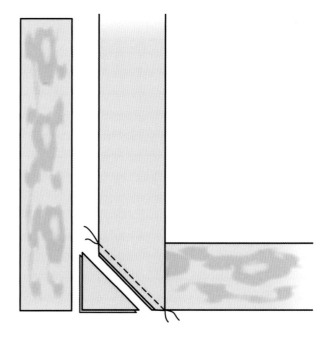

The Quilts

Portugal Strippy

This simple quilt is made of quarter-square triangles and is made using the quilt-as-you-go method, for which a walking foot is an essential requirement for your sewing machine.

Finished size
94 x 112.5 cm/37 x 44¼ in

Materials
All fabrics are 100 per cent cotton.

Body of quilt
    20 squares of fabric, 25.5 cm/10 in (half a Layer Cake pack was used for the front of the quilt)

Backing
    1.4 m/1½ yd

Sashing/Binding
    Co-ordinating colour fabric, 1 m/1 yd

Wadding
    1.2 m/1⅓ yd

CUTTING

1 If you are not using a layer cake cut 20 squares each 25.5 cm/10 in from your chosen fabrics.

2 Cut four strips from the length of the backing fabric, 25.5 x 119.5 cm/10 x 47 in.

3 Cut the wadding into four strips, 25.5 x 119.5 cm/10 x 47 in.

4 From the width of the sashing fabric, cut four strips each 2.75 cm/1⅛ in wide. Cut four more strips each 4.75 cm/1⅞ in wide.

5 From the width of the binding fabric, cut five strips each 6.5 cm/2½ in.

STITCHING

1 Arrange the 20 fabric squares into pairs. Place a pair right sides together and draw a line across the diagonal on the wrong side of one square. Pin, then stitch 7.5 mm/¼ in to each side of this line to make two half-square triangles. Repeat for all ten pairs.

2 Cut the triangles apart on the drawn line, open out and press the seams to one side (diagram 1).

DIAGRAM 1

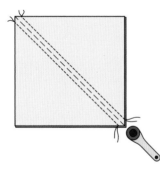

3 Put the right sides of two of the half-square triangle blocks together with the diagonal seamline matching (make sure that the pressed seams are in opposite directions to reduce bulk) and draw a line on the wrong side of the fabric on the opposite diagonal line. Pin, then stitch 7.5 mm/¼ in to each side of this line to yield two quarter-square triangle blocks. Repeat for all ten pairs.

4 Cut the blocks apart on the drawn line (diagram 2). Open out and press the seams. The blocks should measure 23.5 cm/9¼ in square to the raw edge

DIAGRAM 2

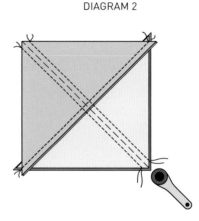

5 Stitch the blocks into four strips of five blocks. Spread one backing strip right side down on a flat surface, then smooth out the wadding. Add the wadding strip and the pieced top strip, right side facing on top. Fasten together with safety pins or baste in a grid (diagram 3).

DIAGRAM 3

6 Hand or machine quilt the layers as desired.

SASHING STRIPS

1 Piece both sets of sashing strips together so that they are long enough for your strips. Stitch together with a diagonal seam and press the seam open.

2 Fold the 4.75 cm/1⁷/₈ in-wide sashing strip in half with the wrong sides together and press.

3 Align the raw edge of the 2.75 cm/ 1¹/₈ in wide sashing strip with the first quilt strip with right sides together. Then place the raw edges of the folded strip on reverse, matching all raw edges. Pin then stitch both sashing strips at the same time to the first quilt strip with a 7.5 mm/¼ in seam (diagram 4).

DIAGRAM4

4 Trim the ends of the sashing strips to match the top and bottom edges of the quilt strip. Pin, then stitch the second quilt strip to the raw edge of the 2.75 cm/1 in-wide sashing strip with right sides facing. Continue joining your quilt and sashing strips in the same way until the four strips are stitched together.

5 Pin the folded edge of each sashing strip on the back of the quilt top in place to cover the seam allowance and slip stitch in place by hand. You can also stitch this in place by machine.

BINDING

1 Join the binding strips with diagonal seams to make a continuous length to fit all around the quilt and use to bind the edges with a double-fold binding, mitred at the corners.

Water's Edge

This simple pattern based on halved layer cakes can be put together very quickly but is still attractive and especially good at showing off the beauty of the fabric itself. Water's Edge was the range of Moda Layer Cake used for this pattern.

Finished size
116 x 178 cm/45½ x 70 in

Materials
All fabrics are 100 per cent cotton.

Body of quilt
   One layer cake packet or 40 different
   25.5 cm/10 in squares

Backing
   If you are using a fabric with a width of
   114 cm/45 in or more you will
   need 2 m/2¼ yd, or you will need to
   join the backing to give you a width of
   4 m/4½ yd

Binding
   Co-ordinating colour fabric,
   45 cm/18 in

Wadding
   50 x 76 in/127 x 193 cm

NOTE If you purchase the wadding in a pack, unpack it and hang it somewhere to allow the creases to drop for 24 hours. Alternatively, open out the wadding and pop it into a tumble dryer on a cool setting for about 10 minutes. Wadding purchased off the roll by the meter/yard does not usually need to be hung and is ready to use.

CUTTING

1 This quilt is made up of 25 blocks. Cut the 40 x 10 in/25.5 cm squares in half to yield 80 rectangles, 12.75 x 25.5 cm/5 x 10 in. Keep the cut squares in order in two piles (diagram 1).

DIAGRAM 1

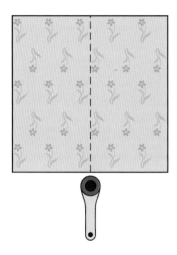

2 If you are not using a layer cake, cut 40 squares, 25.5 x 25.5 cm/10 x 10 in from your chosen fabrics and then cut each in half to yield 80 rectangles, 12.75 x 25.5 cm/ 5 x 10 in. Keep the cut squares in order in two piles (diagram 1).

3 From the binding fabric cut seven strips, 5.5 cm/2¼ in wide, across the width of the fabric.

STITCHING

1 You now have two piles of rectangles. Take the top 10 rectangles from one pile and set aside. Turn one pile over so that the top fabric becomes the bottom fabric. The two piles of fabric will now have one with the right side facing up and one with the wrong side facing up (diagram 2).

DIAGRAM 2

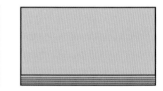

2 Take one rectangle from each pile. With right sides facing, join them together using a 7.5 mm/¼ in seam allowance. Repeat this until you have joined together 25 blocks (diagram 3). Press the seams to one side. Alternatively, you can sort through the two piles of rectangles and pair them up as desired.

DIAGRAM 3

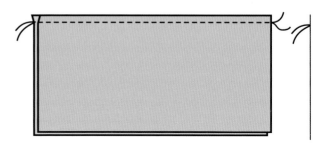

3 You will now have 20 rectangles left. Add the 10 you set aside to this pile. Cut 1.25 cm/½ in off the length to make 12.75 x 24 cm/5 x 9½ in rectangles. Join these rectangles on to the top edge of each previously pieced block. This will make a block 24 x 37 cm/9½ x 14¼ in (diagram 4).

DIAGRAM 4

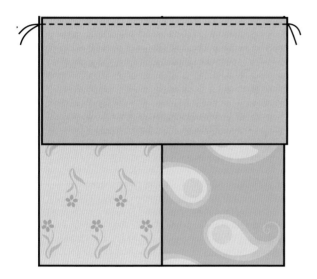

4 The quilt top is made up of five blocks across by five rows down. Take five of the blocks and join them in a row – do this five times. Then join the five rows together.

FINISHING

DIAGRAM 5

1 Measure the quilt top through the centre horizontally and vertically to check your measurements. The quilt top should measure 116 x 178 cm/45½ x 70 in. If the measurements are different from this adjust your wadding and backing fabric to fit.

2 If the backing fabric is not wide enough to fit the quilt top, join the fabric to make one piece measuring at least 127 x 193 cm/ 50 x 76 in taking a 1.25 cm/½ in seam allowance. Press the seam open.

3 Spread the backing right side down on a flat surface making sure that you smooth out any wrinkles then add the wadding and the pieced top, right side up on top. Baste the layers together with safety pins, tack with a tacking gun or hand baste in a grid (diagram 5).

4 Hand or machine stitch the quilt. Join all the binding strips into one length and use to bind the quilt with a double-fold binding, mitred at the corners.

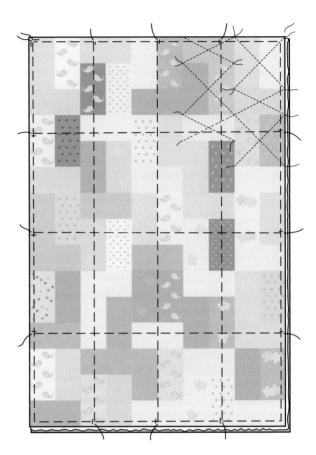

Fan Quilt

This quilt is a great way of displaying all those 1930s-style fabrics and the multi-layered effect of the design gives it depth. There is only one block involved so it couldn't be easier.

Finished size
142.25 cm/56 in square

Materials
All fabrics are 100 per cent cotton.

Body of quilt
    Cream fabric: 2.65 m/2⅞ yd
    18 fat quarters of 1930s-style fabrics

Green fabric for borders and binding
    1 m/1¼ yd

Backing
    163 cm/64 in square

Wadding
    163 cm/64 in square

CUTTING

Cream fabric

Cut 36 squares each 22 cm/8½ in.
Cut 5 squares each 23.5 cm/9¼ in and cut in half diagonally twice for border.
Cut 4 squares each 12.5 cm/4⅞ in and cut in half diagonally once for end of borders.

Green border and binding fabric

Cut 6 squares each 23.5 cm/9¼ in and cut in half diagonally twice for the border.
Cut 4 squares each 11.5 cm/4½ in for the border.
Cut 6 strips 5.5 cm/2¼ in across width of fabric for binding.

Fans from 1930s-style fabric

Cut 216 pieces from template 1. Cut 36 pieces from template 2.

STITCHING

1 Fold each fan segment in half lengthways with right sides together (diagram 1).

DIAGRAM 1

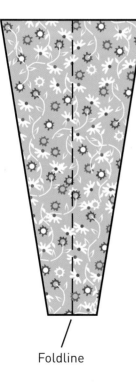

Foldline

2 Stitch a 7.5 mm/¼ in seam across the wider end (diagram 2).

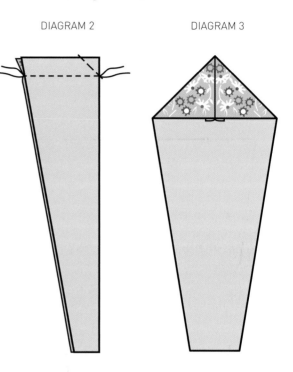

DIAGRAM 2   DIAGRAM 3

3 Clip the corner and unfold. You will now have a piece with a little 'hood' on it (diagram 3 above). Make six for each complete fan; there are 36 fans in all.

4 Choosing randomly from your fabric selection stitch 6 fan shapes together, press the seams open, remembering to press each seam as you go. Repeat until you have 36 fans in all (diagram 4).

DIAGRAM 4

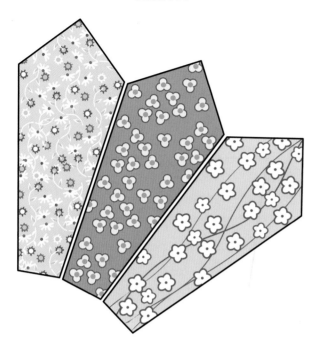

5 To position a fan accurately on the 22 cm/8½ in cream square, first fold the square in half diagonally and lightly fingerpress.

6 Place the centre fan seam over the fold and pin in place. You may occasionally need to trim a fraction off at each side. Appliqué in place using a fine hemming stitch and a toning thread.

7 Now turn under 7.5 mm/¼ in on the curved edge of each quarter circle (template 2) and appliqué over the fan.

8 Using the quilt plan as a guide arrange the blocks in a grid of six blocks wide and 6 deep. Stitch the blocks together in rows and then stitch the rows to make up the quilt front.

BORDERS

The border is made by stitching the triangles together in rows working from left to right and starting and finishing with a small triangle, matching the ends of the border triangles to the edges of the assembled quilt top.

1 Stitch the corner squares to the top and bottom border strips.

2 Stitch the borders to the quilt sides first and then top and bottom.

FINISHING

1 Measure the quilt top through the centre horizontally and vertically to check your measurements and adjust your wadding and backing fabric to fit.

2 Spread the backing right side down on a flat surface, then, working from the centre outwards, smooth out the wadding and the patchwork top, right side up, on top. Fasten together with safety pins or baste in a grid, working from the centre out.

3 Mark the quilting design on the quilt. Hand or machine quilt the layers.

BINDING

Join the binding strips with diagonal seams to make a continuous length to fit all around the quilt and use to bind the edges with a double-fold binding, mitred at the corners.

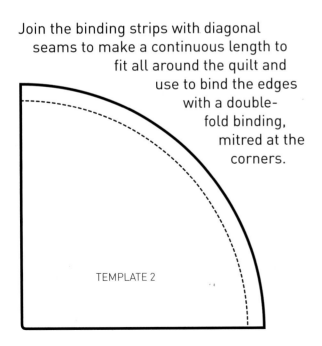

TEMPLATE 2

TIP This quilt was long-arm quilted but you might like to quilt by hand or machine either echoing the fan shapes or with an overall design of flowers and leaves.

Templates are shown at 100 per cent of actual size.

TEMPLATE 1

Quillow

Ideal to keep in the car or caravan, where it can be used as a cushion and opened out to use as a quilt to picnic on or snuggle under.

Finished size
122.5 x 155 cm/48¼ x 61 in

Materials
All fabrics are 100 per cent cotton.

Body of quilt
    Star Centre: 35 cm/³/₈ yd blue pattern
    Star Points, First Border and Binding:
     1.15 m/1¼ yd solid red
    Star Background: ⁷/₈ yd/80 cm yellow
     pattern
    Star Framing: 50 cm/½ yd solid yellow

    Main Fabric and Second Border
     2.1 m/2¼ yd green/blue pattern

Backing
    142.25 x 175.25 cm/56 x 69 in for
    quilt plus a 51 cm/20 in square for
    cushion back

Wadding
    142.25 x 175.25 cm/56 x 69 in for
    quilt plus a 51 cm/20 in square for
    cushion front

CUTTING

This quilt is made up of 13 patchwork blocks – 12 for the main quilt and one for the cushion front – and six plain blocks. Cut four strips 11.5 cm/4½ in down the length of the main fabric for the borders before cutting other shapes.

Star Background (yellow pattern)

Cut 52 rectangles 6.5 x 11.5 cm/ 2½ x 4½ in. Cut 52 squares 6.5 cm/ 2½ in.

Star Points (solid red)

Cut 104 squares 6.5 cm/2½ in.

Star Centre (blue pattern)

Cut 13 squares 11.5 cm/4½ in.

Star Framing (solid yellow)

Cut 26 strips 2.5 x 21.5 cm/1 x 8½ in.
Cut 26 strips 2.5 x 24 cm/1 x 9½ in.

Main Fabric (breen/blue pattern)

Cut six squares 24 cm/9½ in. Cut four squares 19 cm/7½ in, cut on the diagonal once to form corner triangles.

Cut three squares 35cm/14 in, cut on the diagonal twice to form setting triangles.

Binding

Cut 6 strips 6.5 cm/2½ in for main quilt and cushion front across the width of the fabric.

STITCHING

1 Draw a diagonal line on the wrong side of each 6.5 cm/2½ in square of Star Point (solid red) fabric.

2 With right sides together, position a Star Point square on one end of a rectangle of Star Background fabric. Align the raw edges then pin and stitch on the pencil line.

3 Trim away the excess yellow background fabric to 7.5mm/¼ in beyond the stitched line.

4 Press the Star Point triangle back, seam towards the background fabric.

5 Repeat for the other side. The finished unit should measure 6.5 x 11.5 cm/ 2½ x 4½ in.

6 Use the 6.5 cm/2½ in squares of yellow pattern background and the blue pattern squares cut for the star centres to make up 13 (diagram 1) blocks. The finished Star Block should measure 22 cm/8½ in to the raw edge.

DIAGRAM 1

7 Stitch a 2.5 x 22 cm/1 x 8½ in of framing fabric to the top and bottom of each star block.

8 Stitch a 2.5 x 24 cm/1 x 9½ in of framing fabric to either side of the star block. The block should now measure 24 cm/9½ in square.

9 Stitch the blocks together in diagonal rows, alternating patchwork blocks and plain 24 cm/9½ in green/blue pattern squares and adding a setting triangle as shown in the quilt assembly diagram.

To make sure the corners are square find the centre of the corner triangles and match up with the centre of the block (diagram 2).

DIAGRAM 2

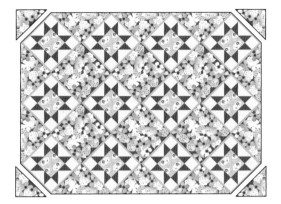

BORDERS

1 The first red border is cut 4 cm/1½ in. Measure the quilt through the width, cut the border fabric to this length, and stitch to the top and bottom edges. Measure the quilt through the length, join the border strips as necessary to make up the length needed, and stitch to each side of the quilt.

2 Measure and stitch the second border as for first border.

FINISHING

1 Measure the quilt top through the centre horizontally and vertically to check your measurements and adjust wadding and backing to fit as necessary.

2 Spread the backing right side down on a flat surface, then, working from the centre outwards, smooth out the wadding and the patchwork top, right side up, on top. Fasten together with safety pins or baste in a grid, working from the centre out.

3 Mark a quilting design on the quilt. Hand or machine quilt the layers.

CUSHION FRONT

1 Stitch corner square triangles to each corner of the remaining star block (diagram 3).

DIAGRAM 3

2 Stitch a 7.5 x 33.75 cm/3 x 13¼ in strip of fabric used for the first border to the top and bottom of the cushion front. Add a 7.5 x 46.5 cm/3 x 18¼ in strip of the same fabric to each side.

3 Place the cushion wadding on a work surface with the square of backing fabric right side facing, then the cushion top right side down. Pin and stitch on three sides, leaving the top edge open.

4 Clip the corners and turn through to the right side. Roll the edges between your fingers to give a good edge and baste all around. Quilt the cushion top as desired.

5 Position the cushion front in the centre of one short edge of the quilt, align the raw edges of the quilt and the cushion; the right side of cushion front will be facing the backing fabric. Tack the raw edges of cushion and quilt together.

BINDING

1 Align the raw edges of the binding with the raw edges of the front of the quilt. Make sure that the cushion front is sewn through when stitching the binding. Join the binding strips with diagonal seams to make a continuous length to fit all around the quilt and use to bind the edges with a double-fold binding, mitred at the corners.

2 Turn the binding to the back, slipstitch into place. Slipstitch two sides of the cushion to the back of the quilt leaving the bottom end open, making sure that the stitches do not come through to the front. A couple of extra stitches will be needed on the two corners for reinforcement.

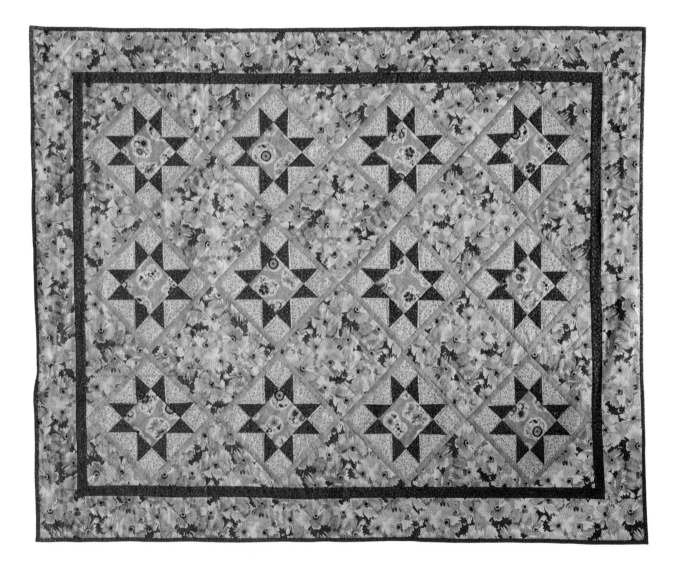

Diamond Quilt

With so many lovely colours in this harlequin of delightful diamonds, this quilt is guaranteed to fit in any room. Make it using fat quarters from your stash. The hues can be bright or muted according to your style.

Finished size
161.25 x 185.5 cm/63½ x 73 in

Materials
All fabrics are 100 per cent cotton.

Body of quilt
   30 fat eighths in a selection of different
   fabrics

Background fabric
   3 m/3¼ yd cream

Backing
   181.5 x 205.75 cm/71½ x 81 in

Binding
   50 cm/½ yd if made using just one
   fabric

Wadding
   181.5 x 205.75 cm/71½ x 81 in

Template plastic

NOTE The binding for this quilt was pieced from leftovers. To do the same you need a finished length of 7.2 m/7⅞ yd made of strips 5.5 cm/2¼ in wide.

TIPS Change your machine needles regularly – this helps to create better stitches and therefore a better quilt.

A multi-coloured thread would blend very well with this quilt.

CUTTING

1 Make up all the templates.

2 Cut 144 pieces each from templates A and B using a random selection of coloured fabrics.

3 Cut 144 pieces from template A using background fabric.

4 Cut 144 pieces from template B using background fabric.

5 Cut 12 pieces from template C using background fabric as setting triangles on the long edge of the quilt.

6 Cut 10 pieces from template D* using background fabric.

7 Cut 2 left pieces from template E and 2 right pieces from template E from the background fabric for the corners.

8 For the border cut enough strips measuring 6.5 x 9 cm/2½ x 3½ in from your coloured fabrics to fit around the quilt's edge.

9 Cut 7 strips 5.5 cm/2¼ in deep across the width of fabric or piece binding to make required length.

STITCHING

There is only one block used in this quilt so it really is very straightforward.

1 Arrange the colours for each block using the quilt plan as a guide.

2 Stitch together one cream background fabric template A patch to a coloured template A patch. Stitch together a cream template B patch to a coloured template B patcg. Stitch the two resulting pieces together to make half the block, press each seam as you go.

3 Repeat to make the other half of the block.

4 Stitch the two halves of the block together and repeat until you have 72 blocks in total (diagram 1).

DIAGRAM 1

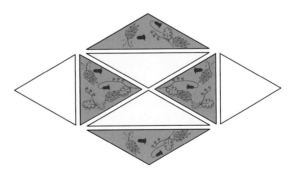

5 Once you have all the blocks made arrange them in diagonal rows in order either using the quilt plan as a guide. Place the background fabric triangles at each end of the diagonal rows.

6 Starting at the top left-hand corner of the quilt, complete the corner first and work across the quilt stitching in diagonal rows, not forgetting to include the end triangles (diagram 2).

DIAGRAM 2

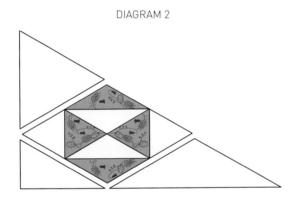

BORDERS

1 Measure the pieced top through the centre from top to bottom, then stitch together in strips enough border rectangles to fit each side and the top and bottom edges.

2 Pin, then stitch the side strips to the quilt.

3 Measure the pieced top through the centre from side to side, then pin and stitch the remaining strips to the top and bottom edges.

FINISHING

1 Measure the quilt top through the centre horizontally and vertically to check your measurements and adjust your wadding and backing fabric to fit.

2 Spread the backing right side down on a flat surface, then, working from the centre outwards, smooth out the wadding and the patchwork top, right side up, on top. Fasten together with safety pins or baste in a grid, working from the centre out.

3 Mark your quilting design on the quilt. Hand or machine quilt the layers.

BINDING

Join the binding strips with diagonal seams to make a continuous length to fit all round the quilt and use to bind the edges with a double-fold binding, mitred at the corners.

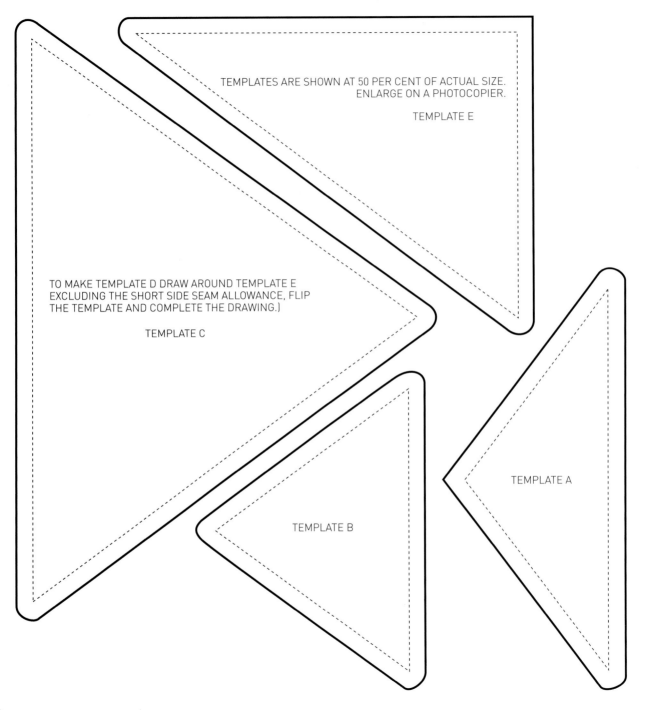

TEMPLATES ARE SHOWN AT 50 PER CENT OF ACTUAL SIZE.
ENLARGE ON A PHOTOCOPIER.

TEMPLATE E

TO MAKE TEMPLATE D DRAW AROUND TEMPLATE E
EXCLUDING THE SHORT SIDE SEAM ALLOWANCE, FLIP
THE TEMPLATE AND COMPLETE THE DRAWING.)

TEMPLATE C

TEMPLATE A

TEMPLATE B

Twinkling Star

Make this soft throw or bed quilt using triangles from squares and see for yourself how easy it is. You can also pick up some tips on organizing your work-in-progress to ensure a successful result. Surround the completed blocks with narrow sashing strips and a simple wide border.

Finished size
163 x 163 cm/64 x 64 in

Materials
All fabrics are 100 per cent cotton.

Stars
    Various plaids, scraps to total 1.2 m/
    $1^1/_3$ yd (For one star you will need at
    least 12.5 x 18 cm/5 x 7 in.)

Block backgrounds
    Natural calico 2.25 m/2½ yd

Narrow sashings
    Striped fabric 60 cm/$^2/_3$ yd

Wide outer border
    Co-ordinating plaid 1.9 m/2 yd

Binding and backing
    3.6 m/3$^7/_8$ yd

Wadding
    180 x 180 cm/68 x 68 in

Gridded interfacing: 2.5 m/2½ yd

CUTTING

Remove any selvages before cutting.

1 From plaid fabric scraps, cut strips 4 cm/1½ in deep, across the width of the fabric. Cross-cut these into 4 cm/1½ in squares. For each of the 36 stars you will need 6 squares, making a total of 216. On the wrong side of these squares use a ruler and marking pencil to draw a diagonal line from corner to corner.

2 From calico, cut 23 strips each 9.5 cm/3½ in deep across the width of the fabric. Cross-cut each strip into 10 squares each 9.5 cm/3½ in, to yield 230 squares. Discard five.

3 For the sashing, from striped fabric, cut 10 strips across the width of the fabric and 3.5 cm/1¼ in deep.

4 For the outer border, from co-ordinating plaid, cut four strips each 21.5 cm/8½ in wide down the length of the fabric, parallel to the selvages. Trim two of the border strips to 129.5 cm/48½ in long and the remaining two to 169.5 cm/64½ in.

5 Cut the backing fabric into two lengths each 180 cm/68 in. From each length cut two strips 6 cm/2½ in wide down the full length of the fabric for the binding.

STITCHING

1 Before you start stitching you will need to decide which "star" fabrics to combine in each block from the plaid fabric scraps. Using the gridded interfacing, pin the squares together in possible combinations of nine blocks each featuring four stars. Each of the nine blocks is made up of 25 calico squares as follows: 4 units have two different plaid fabric scraps (A), 4 units have two of the same plaid fabric triangles (B), 8 units have one plaid fabric triangle (C) and the remaining 9 units are plain calico (diagram 1).

DIAGRAM 1

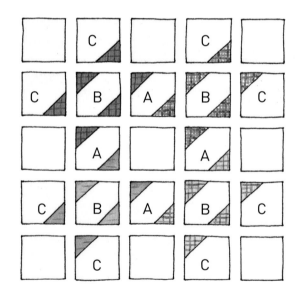

2 Decisions made, remove the squares from the interfacing but pin the units together with safety pins until they are required. Work on one quilt block at a time. Pin 25 calico squares to the interfacing, setting them five squares across by five squares down. Fold the small plaid squares into triangle shapes and, using the diagram as a guide, pin them to the background squares in the appropriate places (diagram 2). Make sure they are all pointing in the right directions.

DIAGRAM 2

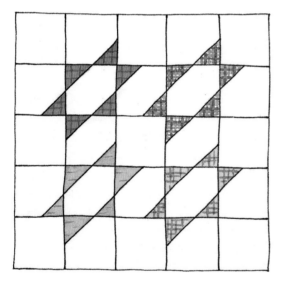

3 Working on one background square at a time, remove it with the star fabric(s) and stitch the triangle(s) in place individually. It is easiest to stitch the four squares with two different star fabrics first, then the four which had matching star fabrics. Finally, chain-piece the eight squares, which have only one star triangle each.

4 Return each unit to its proper place on the interfacing after it is stitched. Stitch the calico squares into five strips of five squares each. Press the seams of strips one, three and five to the right, and two and four to the left. Stitch the strips together to form the completed block. Press the long seams open to reduce the bulk. Complete all nine blocks in this way.

5 Take two sashing strips, place them right sides together and stitch across the narrow width of the strip. If you are using a striped fabric, carefully match and pin so that the seam line falls along the edge of the stripe and is hidden. Repeat three more times. Press the seams open.

6 Arrange the strips out flat. Using a measuring tape, measure off 64.75 cm/24½ in to the left and to the right of the seam line. Mark and cut the sashing at those points, giving you a pieced sashing 129.5 cm/48½ in long. Repeat three more times.

7 From the remnants, cut 8 shorter strips, each 41.5 cm/15½ in long. Cross-cut two more shorter pieces 41.5 cm/15½ in long from each of the remaining two long lengths. You should now have 12 short and four long sashing strips.

8 Arrange 9 completed blocks into the quilt top. Place the three top blocks near your sewing machine. Stitch a short sash to the right-hand side of each block, right sides together (diagram 3). Stitch the fourth sash to the left-hand side of the first block.

DIAGRAM 3

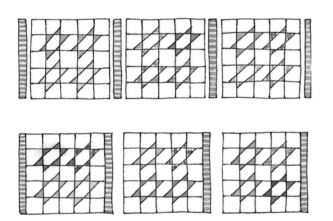

9 Flip the second block over the first, right sides together, and stitch the seam between the sash and the second block. Add the third block in the same way. Complete the remaining two strips in the same fashion. Press all seams towards the sashing.

10 Pin and stitch a long pieced sashing strip to both edges of the top strip. Pin and stitch the remaining two long pieced sashing strips to the lower edges of the middle and bottom strips. Pin and stitch both top and bottom strips to the middle one. Press the seams towards the sashing (diagram 4).

DIAGRAM 4

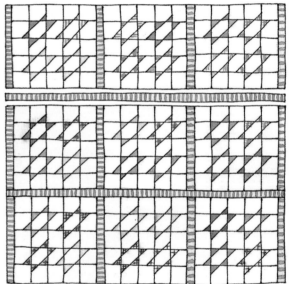

11 Fold and mark the midpoint and the quarter points of the short side border strips and the sides of the quilt. Matching the markings, pin and stitch the right-hand border to the quilt. Repeat for the left-hand border. Press seams towards the sashing. Repeat this process for the top and bottom borders.

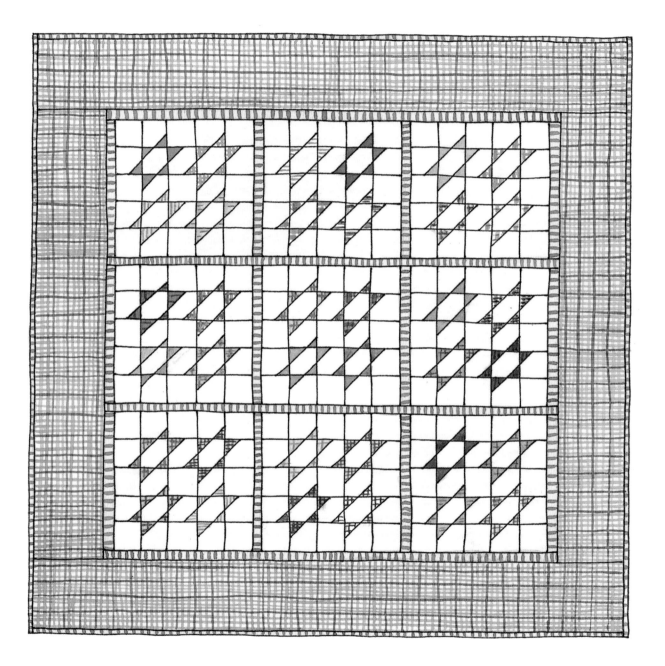

FINISHING

DIAGRAM 5

1 Stitch the two lengths of backing fabric right sides together. Press the seam to one side.

2 Arrange the backing, right side down, on a large flat surface with the wadding on top. Centre the quilt, right side up, over the backing and wadding. Smooth all layers making sure there are no wrinkles. Using a long needle and a light coloured thread, tack the quilt layers together.

3 Using a marker and a quilter's quarter, mark the quilting lines 7.5 mm/¼ in outside of all the stars and the same amount inside the centres. Mark straight lines around the borders, 8 cm/3 in and 13 cm/ 5 in from the narrow striped border. Hand quilt along the marked lines (diagram 5).

4 Trim the edges of the quilt and square up the corners. Using the binding strips, bind the edges of your quilt with a double straight binding.

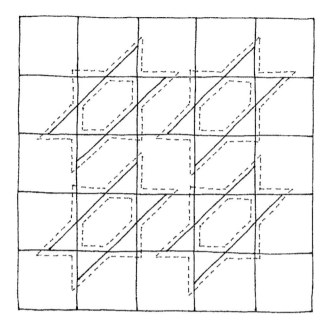

Squares and Stars

A variety of reproduction 1930s prints make up the scrappy sixteen-patch blocks, which are speedily put together using strip cutting and chain-piecing methods. Easy stitch-and-flip stars add interest to the sashing. The blocks are large, measuring 10 in/26 cm when finished, so this double-bed quilt grows quickly.

Finished size
214.5 x 279.5 cm/82½ x 107½ in

Materials
All fabrics used are 100 per cent cotton.

Blocks
    22 fat or long quarter yards or metres or equivalent in scraps

Sashing
    White: 4 m/3½ yd

Stars and binding
    Red: 2 m/2¼ yd

Backing
    6 m/6½ yd in colour of your choice

Wadding (Batting)
    305 x 305 cm/120 x 120 in

NOTE: You will need the equivalent of 768 x 8 cm/3 in squares and a fat or long quarter should yield 42 squares.

CUTTING

1 From the block fabrics, cut strips across the width of the fabric, 8 cm/3¼ in deep, for the 16-patch blocks. If you are cutting from long quarters, cut the strips of fabric in half so that you are working with strips measuring 8 cm/3¼ in x approximately 53 cm/21 in.

2 From the white sashing fabric, cut 35 strips across the width of the fabric, 8 cm/3¼ in deep. Cross-cut the strips into 27.75 cm/10½ in rectangles (see Note). You will need 140 rectangles. Take two of the rectangles and crosscut them to give four 8 cm/3¼ in squares for the outer corners of the quilt top. Cut two additional strips across the width of the fabric, 8 cm/ 3¼ in deep, and cross-cut them to give 28 squares each 8 cm/3¼ in for use in the outer border.

> NOTE: If making the metric version, cut 46 strips and cut the 8 cm/3 in squares from the offcuts after cutting the 27.75 cm/ 10½ in rectangles.

3 From the red star fabric, cut five strips across the width of the fabric, 8 cm/3¼in deep. Cross-cut the strips into 63 squares each 8 cm/3 in for the centres of the stars. Cut 22 strips, 4.75 cm/1¾ in deep and crosscut these into 504 squares each 1¾ in/4.75 cm for the star points. Cut eight strips, 6 cm/2½ in deep across the width of the remaining red fabric for the binding.

STITCHING

1 With right sides facing and taking a 7.5 mm/¼ in seam allowance, stitch the strips of fabric for the blocks into random pairs along the length of the strips. Chain piecing the strips will save time and thread. Press carefully, pressing the seam joining the strips "flat" or closed first, then flipping the top strip over and pressing from the front to ensure the seam is smooth.

2 Taking a 7.5 mm/¼ in seam allowance, join pairs of strips to make 32 strip sets of four fabrics with as much variety in the combinations of fabrics as possible. Press the seams as before.

3 Cut the strip sets into sections 8 cm/ 3¼ in wide (diagram 1). Each strip set should yield 6 sections.

DIAGRAM 1

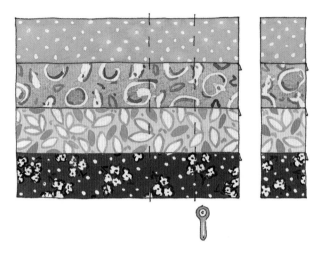

4 Taking a 7.5 mm/¼ in seam allowance, stitch four sections together to make a 16-patch block, which should measure 26.5 cm/10½ in at this stage (diagram 2).

DIAGRAM 2

5 Make 48 blocks in all. The more fabrics you have included in different combinations, the easier it will be to vary the composition of each block and achieve the scrappy look of the quilt.

6 Prepare the sashing. Take 28 of the rectangles and four 8 cm/3¼ in squares of sashing fabric and set them aside for the outer border.

7 Draw a diagonal pencil line across the wrong side of each of the red 4.75 cm/1¾ in squares. Place one square on the corner of one sashing rectangle, right sides together and stitch along the drawn diagonal line. Press the square flat first to set the seam, then press the triangular flap of the square out towards the corner of the sashing rectangle: if you have stitched accurately, the triangle will fit perfectly into the corner of the sashing rectangle.

8 Trim away the excess fabric (diagram 3a).

DIAGRAM 3A

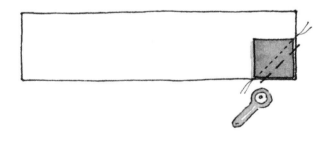

9 Stitch another red square on to the adjacent corner (diagram 3b). Repeat for the other two corners of the sashing rectangle, then repeat for all 110 rectangles.

DIAGRAM 3B

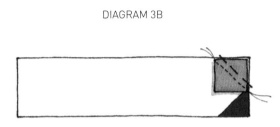

10 Following the quilt plan, arrange the completed 16-patch blocks in eight rows of six blocks. Taking a 7.5 mm/¼ in seam allowance, stitch a sashing strip to the right-hand edge of each block and also to the left-hand edge of the first block in each row. Pin and stitch the blocks into rows and press well with the seams towards the blocks.

11 Taking a 7.5 mm/¼ in seam allowance, stitch six sashing strips together with a star centre square between each strip and at each end. Press the seam allowances towards the star centres. Pin the long sashing strip to fit between the first two rows of the quilt top, matching seams, and stitch carefully. Press the seam allowances towards the sashing.

12 Join the remaining rows of blocks, alternating with sashing, in the same way, and stitch a row of sashing to the top and bottom of the quilt top. Press the quilt top well.

ADDING THE BORDERS

1 The final borders will complete the stars on the outer edges of the design. Take 28 white 8 cm/3¼ in sashing squares and, using the same technique of stitching across the diagonal, add two small red star points to adjacent corners of each square. Press and trim away the excess fabric as before.

2 Taking a 7.5 mm/¼ in seam allowance, stitch nine of these units together with eight of the plain sashing rectangles (see quilt plan), then stitch the border to one side of the quilt, matching seams and star points as shown in the quilt assembly diagram. Repeat for the other side border.

3 Make the top and bottom border strips in the same way with the remaining 12 plain sashing rectangles alternating with the 14 squares to which the outer star points have been added, and starting and finishing the borders with the four plain 8 cm/3¼ in sashing squares (diagram 4 shows a detail of the corner of the quilt). Stitch to the top and bottom of the quilt and press well with the seam allowances towards the outer borders.

DIAGRAM 4

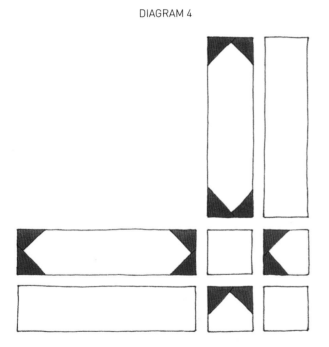

FINISHING

1 Measure the completed patchwork top and cut and piece the backing to fit with at least 5 cm/2 in all round. If you are joining the backing, don't forget to cut off the selvages as these are very tightly woven and can cause distortion in the quilt. Press the seam open.

2 Spread the backing right side down on a flat surface, then smooth out the wadding and the patchwork top, right side up, on top. Fasten together with safety pins or baste in a grid.

3 Mark the top with the desired quilting design and hand or machine quilt.

4 Join the binding strips with diagonal seams to make a continuous length to fit all around the quilt and use to bind the edges with a double-fold binding, mitred at the corners.

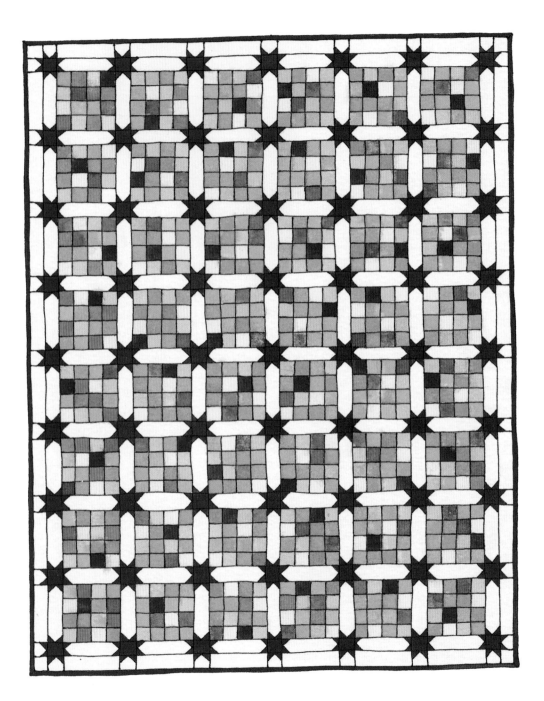

Hidden Stars

Sew this quilt from scraps of your favourite colour – the more different fabrics, the better – but be sure to keep to one colour! There are no tricky triangles to cut, and the "cut and flip" method used ensures accuracy. Because of the diversity of fabrics used, and because they are all the same colour, the pattern creates the optical effect of an Ohio Star moving over the quilt. A border of four fabrics adds to the scrappy look of this stunning quilt.

Finished size
152.5 x 152.5cm/60 x 60 in

Materials
All fabrics used are 100 per cent cotton.

Main feature blue fabric
Various blue fabrics: scraps to total
2.2 m/2 yd 6 in (You must be able to cut
a square 16 cm/6½ in from each scrap.)

Alternate fabric
Bleached calico: 2.2 m/2 yd 6 in

Border
Four different blue fabrics (preferably
those that have been used in the quilt),
40 cm/15 in of each

Binding
One of the blue fabrics, 40 cm/15 in

Backing
178 x 178 cm/70 x 70 in

Wadding
178 x 178 cm/70 x 70 in

CUTTING

1 From the blue fabrics, cut 6 strips 16 cm/6½ in wide. Cross-cut each strip into 16 cm/6½ in squares. You will need 32.

2 From the blue fabrics, cut 11 strips 8 cm/3½ in wide. Cross-cut each strip into 8 cm/3½ in squares. You will need 128. On the wrong side of each square, use a ruler and marking pencil to draw a diagonal line from corner to corner.

3 From calico, cut 6 strips 16 cm/6½ in wide. Cross-cut each strip into 16 cm/6½ in wide squares. You will need 32.

4 From calico, cut 11 strips 8 cm/3½ in wide. Cross-cut each strip into 8 cm/3½ in squares. You will need 128. On the wrong side of each square, draw a diagonal line from corner to corner.

5 From the blue fabric for the border, cut 2 strips from 4 different fabrics 16 cm/6½ in wide, trimming off the selvages.

6 From the binding fabric, cut 7 strips 5.5 cm/2¼ in wide.

STITCHING

1 To sew the blocks with dark centres, collect the large blue squares and the small calico squares. Place a calico square wrong-side up in the top left-hand corner of a large blue square, right sides together. Ensure that the drawn line on the calico square runs from one side of the blue square to the top side (diagram 1). Now sew along the drawn line.

DIAGRAM 1

2 Repeat this process on the opposite corner of the large blue square (diagram 2).

DIAGRAM 2

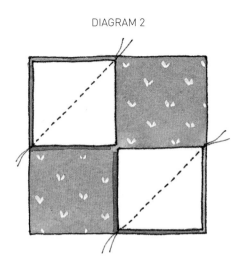

4 Repeat this process on the remaining two corners. When you have finished, all the corners that were originally blue should now be white (diagram 4). Repeat this process using all of the blue squares to make 32 of these blocks.

DIAGRAM 4

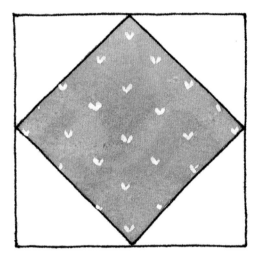

3 Using your ruler and rotary cutter, trim off the corner triangles 5 mm/¼ in from the sewing line. Fold the triangles back to re-form the original square. Press the seam allowance towards the blue fabric (diagram 3).

DIAGRAM 3

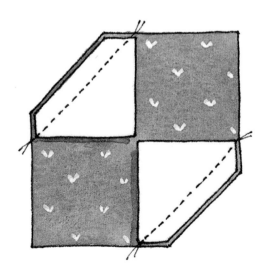

5 To sew the blocks with white centres, collect the large calico squares and the small blue squares. Repeat the process explained in steps 1–4 above, again making 32 of these blocks. If possible, use four different blues on each calico square, as this will maximize the optical effect of the Ohio Star block that will come and go when the quilt is complete. When pressing the seams, press towards the blue corner triangles, as this will help to ensure accuracy when assembling the quilt top.

6 Following the quilt plan, arrange the blocks on a flat surface (use the floor if this is convenient). Start with a dark-centred block in the top left-hand corner and place a light-centred block next to it, continuing along the row alternating blocks. Begin the second row with a light-centred block and again, continue along the row alternating blocks. Build up eight rows in this way using eight blocks per row.

7 Sew the blocks together row by row. As you sew, the blocks should fit neatly together, and the points should all match because of the way you pressed the blocks. Once the first row is sewn, press the seams towards the blocks with the light centres. Continue to press towards these blocks when sewing the rest of the rows, as this will help the straight seams sit together snugly, and your points will all match because of the previous pressing technique.

8 When all of the rows are completed and pressed, sew them together starting at the top of the quilt and working down. When sewing the first two rows together, insert a pin at each straight seam junction and where the points meet (diagram 5). Again, the points and seams should easily match because of the pressing. When all of the rows are sewn together, press all seams in one direction.

DIAGRAM 5

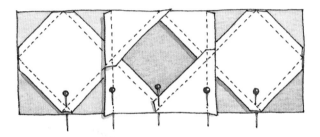

9 Take two strips of the same border fabric and sew them together along the short ends to form one long strip. Press the seam open. Repeat with the remaining border strips. Select the first two borders to be sewn on and place them on opposite sides of the quilt. Trim each of the long strips to 123 cm/48½ in long. Pin and sew the borders to the opposite sides of the quilt, pressing the seams towards the border. Now measure the remaining two strips and cut to 151 cm/60½ in. Pin and sew in place, pressing the seams to the border.

FINISHING

1 Arrange the backing fabric right side down on a large flat surface with the wadding on top. Centre the quilt, right-side up, over the backing and wadding. Carefully smooth all three layers, making sure there are no wrinkles. Using a long needle and a light coloured thread, tack the quilt layers together.

2 Using the 7.5 mm/¼ in masking tape, mark out three or four Ohio Stars at random places on the quilt, 7.5 mm/¼ in in from the seams. Hand-quilt the pattern along the marked lines. Now, using the template, cover the remainder of the quilt with the flower motif (diagram 6).

DIAGRAM 6

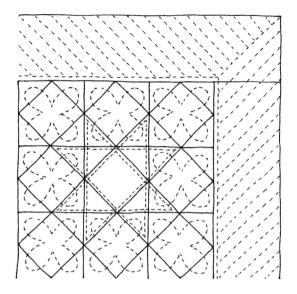

3 Mark a straight line inside the border 5 mm/¼ in away from the seam to frame the centre of the quilt. Using a ruler and Hera marker, mark parallel lines 2.5 cm/ 1 in apart at a 45 degree angle, stretching the width of the border (diagram 6). Hand-quilt along the marked lines.

4 Trim the edges of the quilt and square up the corners. Using the binding strips, bind the edges of your quilt with a double binding with mitred corners.

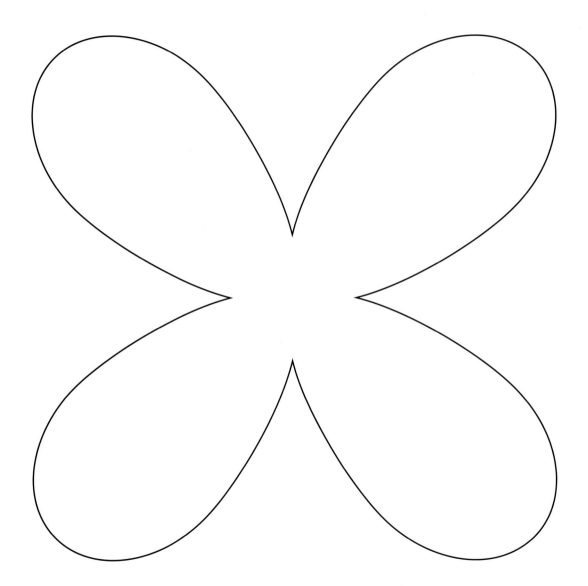

Row of Flowers

This pretty multi-coloured quilt echoes the planted rows of annuals in a summer garden. The soft pastel prints are fenced in by the green of the sashing strips and square corner posts in this trouble-free garden, which will give you pleasure all year round.

Finished size
130 x 130 cm/51 x 51 in

Materials
Remove all selvages before measuring and cutting fabrics.

For the blocks
16 assorted floral prints, 25 cm/¼ yd each

For the blocks and corner posts
5 assorted plain pastel fabrics; one to match the fabric for the sashing strips, 25 cm/¼ yd each

Sashing strips
Green floral print fabric, 90 cm/1 yd

Wadding
55 x 55 in (146 x 146 cm)

Main backing
Small multi-coloured floral print, 1.5 m/1²/₃ yd

Second backing
Tone-on-tone stripe, 1.1 m/1¹/₈ yd

Binding
60 cm/²/₃ yd

CUTTING

1 From one of the floral fabrics for the blocks, cut 3 strips 5.5 cm/2 in deep, across the width of the fabric. Stack up the three strips so that all the edges match and cross-cut them into two lengths of 26.5 cm/10½ in and three lengths of 14.5 cm/5¾ in (diagram 1). Set aside any scraps to use in the blocks if long enough.

DIAGRAM 1

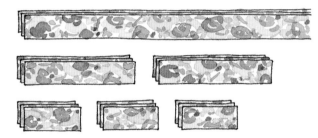

2 Repeat step 1 above for each of the remaining 15 floral fabrics.

3 From the plain fabric that matches the sashing, cut 3 strips 5.5 cm/2 in deep, across the width of the fabric. Stack up the strips as before and cross-cut into 5.5 cm/2 in squares, one length of 26.5 cm/10½ in and three lengths of 14.5 cm/5¾ in. From the remainder of one of the strips, cross-cut one more 5.5 cm/2 in square to yield 16 squares (diagram 2).

DIAGRAM 2

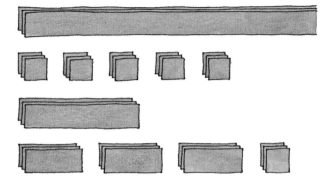

4 Set these aside for the corner posts. Any remaining pieces of strip may be used in the blocks if long enough.

5 Cut the remaining four pastel fabrics as you did the floral ones.

6 From the green floral print fabric for the sashing strips, cut 12 strips 5.5 cm/2 in deep, across the width of the fabric. From each of these strips cut two lengths 41.5 cm/15½ in long.

7 From the main backing fabric, cut three strips 48 cm/18 in deep, across the width of the fabric. Cross-cut each strip into two 48 cm/18 in squares. Discard one square.

8 From the second backing fabric, cut the two strips 48 cm/18 in deep across the width of the fabric. Cross-cut each strip into two 48 cm/18 in squares.

9 From the binding fabric, cut six strips 6 cm/2 ½in deep, across the width of the fabric.

STITCHING

1 Stitch the floral and plain pastel lengths together at random to form a long continuous strip (diagram 3). You may find it easier to work on a few long lengths at a time, joining them all at the end.

DIAGRAM 3

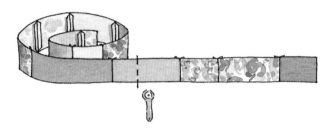

2 To make the blocks, trim the long continuous strip into shorter sections of 41.5 cm (15½ in). You will need 90 lengths: 10 for each block.

3 Choose 10 sections to make up a block and arrange them in front of you. If it looks like any of the short cross-seams in adjacent rows will intersect, press one of the seams in the opposite direction. Stitch the sections together in progressive pairs until the block is complete. Press the long seams in one direction. Repeat for each block.

4 Arrange the blocks on a large, flat surface and decide on their final placement.

5 Stitch the blocks and sashing strips together into three rows of three blocks and four sashing strips each. Press all seams towards the sashing strips. Stitch the alternating rows, consisting of three sashing strips and four corner posts (diagram 4). Press all seams away from the corner posts.

DIAGRAM 4

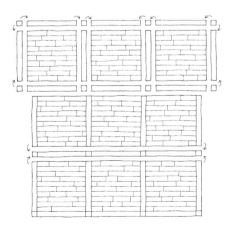

6 Stitch the final long seams, pinning and matching all intersecting seams.

7 Piece the large squares for the backing into what is essentially a giant nine-patch block, pressing intersecting seams on each row in alternate directions and the two final seams in the same direction.

8 Stitch the binding strips into a continuous binding.

FINISHING

1 Measure your pieced backing and cut the wadding to the same size.

2 On a large, flat surface, spread out the wadding and spray baste. Smooth the pieced backing onto the wadding, ensuring there are no wrinkles. Turn the wadding and backing over, spray baste the other side of the wadding and carefully centre the quilt top on the wadding, ensuring there are no wrinkles. Place a few pins in the top for extra strength.

3 Quilt diagonally across the blocks, and outline quilt around the sashing strips (diagram 5).

4 Bind the quilt with the continuous binding, mitring the corners as you go.

DIAGRAM 5

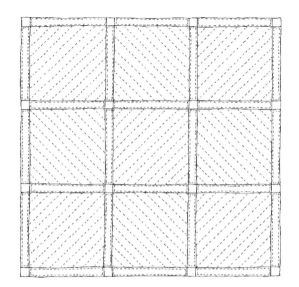

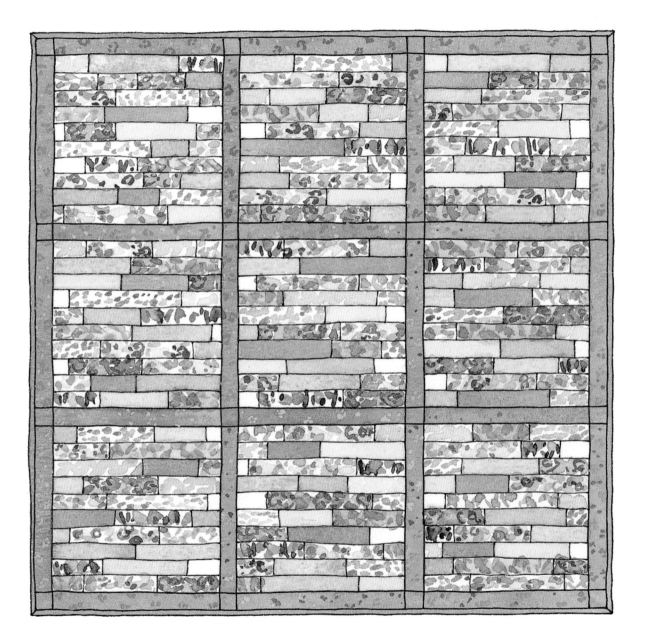

Sister's Choice

Many of the traditional American blocks have more than one name. In addition to "Sister's Choice", this one is also known as "Farmer's Daughter". Whatever the name, the pieced five-patch blocks, in a selection of contemporary prints and set on point with alternate cream setting squares, will make an elegant double-bed quilt for a summer bedroom.

Finished size
93 x 109 in/233 x 272 cm

Materials
All fabrics are 100 per cent cotton.

Blocks, Border, Side Triangles and
Corner Triangles
    Cream all-over print: 7 m/7½ yd

Blocks
    Five harmonizing patterned prints:
    50 cm/24 in of each

Backing
    257 x 298 cm/101 x 117 in in colour of
    your choice

Wadding
    257 x 298 cm/101 x 117 in

Binding
    Additional 75 cm/32 in of one of the
    five harmonizing patterned prints

CUTTING

1 From the cream fabric, cut two strips, 18 x 209 cm/7 x 82 in, and two strips, 18 x 282 cm/7 x 110 in, for the border.

2 From the cream fabric, cut 20 squares each 28.5 cm/11¼ in for the alternate squares.

3 From the cream fabric, cut four squares each 44 cm/17¼ in and cross-cut these into four triangles by cutting across both diagonals. Use one of these triangles as a template to cut two more triangles (18 side triangles).

4 From the cream fabric, cut two 23 cm/9 in squares and cross-cut these into two triangles each by cutting across one diagonal (for the four corner triangles).

STITCHING

1 For the patchwork blocks, from across the width of one of the print fabrics, cut two strips, 8 cm/3⅛ in deep, and three strips, 7 cm/2¾ in deep. Cut the same from the cream fabric. Take one cream and one patterned strip, 7 cm/2¾ in deep and trim to 104 cm/41 in long. Place these two strips right sides together and, taking a 7.5 mm/¼ in seam allowance, stitch along one long side. Cross-cut into 12 segments each 7 cm/2¾ in (diagram 1).

DIAGRAM 1

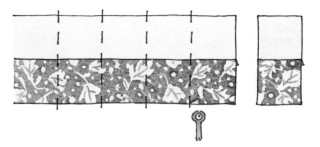

2 From the 7 cm/2¾ in print strips, cut three strips 46 cm/18 in long. From the 7 cm/2¾ in cream fabric strips, cut two lengths 46 cm/18 in long. Stitch these together in the sequence: print/cream/print/cream/print. Cross-cut into six 7 cm/2¾ in segments (diagram 2).

DIAGRAM 2

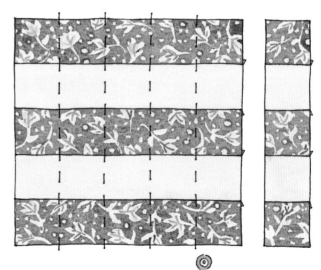

3 From the remaining cream fabric, cut 24 squares each 7 cm/2¾. From the remaining print fabric, cut 24 squares each 7 cm/2¾ in.

4 From the 8 cm/3⅛ in strips, cut six cream and six print strips, 35.5 cm/14 in long. With right sides together, pair up each cream strip with one of the print strips. On the wrong side of each cream strip, mark off four 8 cm/3⅛ in squares. Then draw a continuous zig-zag line from corner to corner of the marked squares along the length of the strip. Stitch along both sides of these lines, 7.5mm/¼ in away (diagram 3a).

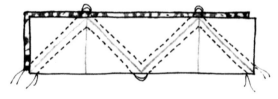

5 Cut along the marked vertical and diagonal lines. Press the seams of the resulting half-square triangle units towards the print side and trim off the small "ears" of fabric that extend beyond the square (total of 48 units) (diagram 3b).

6 Following diagram 4, pin and stitch two of the half-square triangle units, one print 7 cm/2¾ in square and one cream 7 cm/2¾ in square to make the corner sections for the blocks (total of 24 corner sections).

DIAGRAM 4

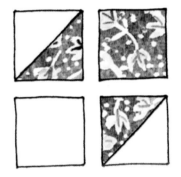

NOTE: You can stitch in a continuous line, using a 7.5 mm/¼ in foot on your sewing machine. If you do not have this facility, mark the sewing line before stitching.

7 Arrange the first block in the sequence shown in diagram 5 as follows: four corner sections, two two-square segments (see step 1) and one five-square segment (see step 2). Taking a 7.5 mm/¼ in seam allowance, pin and stitch the block together as illustrated, keeping the orientation of the seams correct. Make five more blocks from the remaining units.

DIAGRAM 5

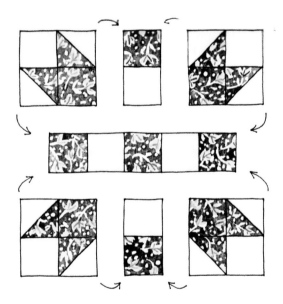

8 Repeat steps 1–7, using the remaining print fabrics combined with the cream fabric to make a total of 30 blocks.

9 Press the pieced blocks thoroughly. If necessary, trim the alternate setting squares, previously cut from the cream fabric, to fit the pieced blocks.

10 Following the quilt plan, arrange the blocks in diagonal rows, alternating the pieced and plain squares. Change the positioning of the pieced blocks until you are happy with the arrangement.

11 Pin and stitch the pieced blocks alternating with the cream squares into diagonal rows, adding the corner and side triangles as you work (diagram 6). Press the seams towards the cream squares. Then pin and stitch the rows together, matching the seams.

DIAGRAM 6

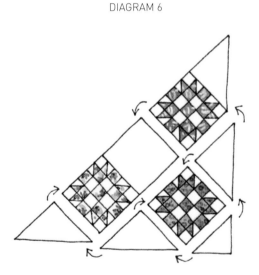

ADDING THE BORDERS

1 Measure the pieced top through the centre from side to side, then trim the two shorter cream border strips to this measurement. Taking a 7.5 mm/¼ in seam allowance, pin and stitch to the top and bottom of the quilt.

2 Measure the pieced top through the centre from top to bottom, then trim the remaining two cream border strips to this measurement. Taking 7.5 mm/¼ in allowance, pin and stitch to each side of the quilt.

FINISHING

1 Spread the backing right side down on a flat surface, then smooth out the wadding and the patchwork top, right side up, on top. Fasten together with safety pins or baste in a grid.

2 Using machine quilting thread, quilt over the surface of the quilt with "free motion" quilting.

3 Trim off any excess wadding and backing level with the pieced top. Using the extra print fabric, cut ten strips, 7 cm/2¾ in wide. Join the binding strips with diagonal seams to make a continuous length to fit around the quilt and use to bind the edges with a double-fold binding, mitred at the corners.

Spider's Web

This string-pieced cot quilt puts narrow scraps of fabric to good use, so it has great design potential for quilters with an organized stash of scrap fabrics. The strips are stitched onto a foundation fabric to produce bigger, more manageable units.

Finished size
32 x 42 in/82 x 108 cm

Materials
All fabrics are 100 per cent cotton.

For the background
White: 1.2 m/1¹/₃ yd

For the spider's webs
Printed fabrics in a selection of bright colours to total 1.5 m 1²/₃ yd (11 different patterns were used here)

Binding
Striped fabric: 30 cm/24 in

Backing
96 x 122 cm/38 x 48 in

Wadding (Batting)
96 x 122 cm/38 x 48 in

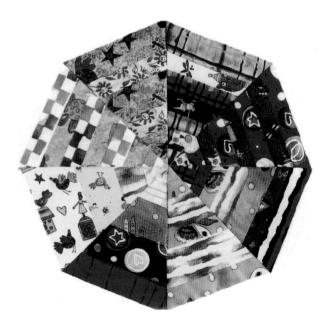

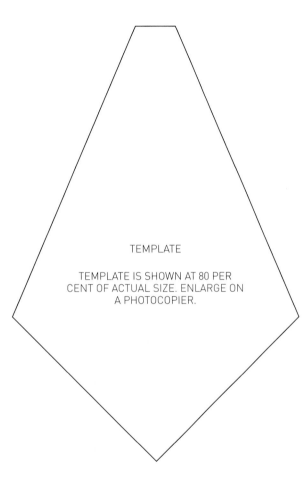

TEMPLATE

TEMPLATE IS SHOWN AT 80 PER
CENT OF ACTUAL SIZE. ENLARGE ON
A PHOTOCOPIER.

CUTTING

1 From white background fabric, cut
24 squares each 22 cm/8½ in. Cut these
in half on the diagonal to make
48 foundation triangles.

2 Cut the printed fabric into strips across
the width of the fabric, varying the depth
from 2.5–5 cm/1–2 in.

3 Cut the binding fabric into four strips,
6.5 cm/2½ in deep, across the width of the
fabric. Fingerpress the strip toward the
point.

4 Trace the template provided onto
template plastic and cut out.

STITCHING THE BLOCKS

1 Place the template on one of the
foundation triangles, aligning the right
angles, and mark along the edge of the
template with a pencil.

2 From one of the strips of printed fabric,
cut a piece about 14 cm/5 in long and
line it up against the marked line on the
foundation triangle, right sides together.
Stitch, taking a 7.5 mm/¼ in seam
allowance (diagram 1).

DIAGRAM 1

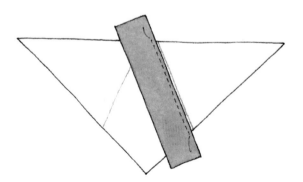

3 Cut the next strip from a different fabric long enough to extend slightly beyond the sides of the foundation triangle. Align with the edge of the first strip, right sides together, and stitch in place. Flip open and fingerpress towards the point. Continue the process until the end of the foundation triangle is covered completely (diagram 2).

DIAGRAM 2

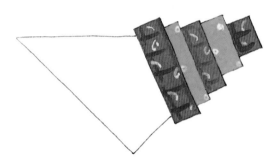

4 Work on the other side of the foundation triangle in the same way, lining up the first strip against the marked line and stitching with an accurate 7.5 mm/¼ in seam (diagram 3).

DIAGRAM 3

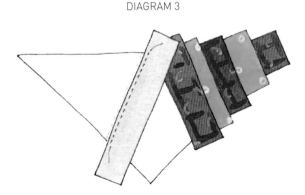

5 Press the triangle when both sides are covered. Place right side down on a cutting board and trim the strips even with the sides of the foundation triangle. Repeat to make a total of 48 triangle units.

6 Stitch four triangle units together to form a block, being careful to match up the points where the strips meet to create the edge of the spider's web (diagram 4).

DIAGRAM 4

NOTE It is important to stitch an accurate 7.5 mm/¼ in seam allowance when you attach the first strip to the foundation triangle, so that the outside edges of the spider's web match up when joined later.

7 Press the seams open to distribute the bulk. Repeat to make a total of 12 blocks.

8 Following the quilt assembly diagram, stitch three blocks together to form a row, then stitch the rows together to complete the pieced top.

FINISHING

1 Spread the backing right side down on a flat surface, then smooth out the wadding and the patchwork top, right side up, on top. Fasten together with safety pins or baste in a grid.

2 Quilt 7.5 mm/¼ in from the seamline on the background fabric and inside the segments of the spider's web. Trim the excess wadding and backing level with the pieced top.

3 Join the binding strips with diagonal seams to make a continuous length to fit all round the quilt and use to bind the edges with a double-fold binding, mitred at the corners.

Jacob's Ladder

Jacob's Ladder is a traditional quilt block that offers easy construction and infinite design possibilities. This version emphasizes the diagonal nature of the block. The fabrics, set against the white background, suggest over-sized candy wrappers.

Finished size
140 x 180 cm/56½ x 72½ in

Materials
All fabrics used are 100 per cent cotton.

For the background and sashing
　　White on white fabric: 2 m/2⅓ yd

For the blocks and sashing posts
　　Four bright prints in blue, yellow, green and pink: 1.9 m/2 yd

For the border and binding
　　An extra 1 m/1 yd of the blue print

Wadding (Batting)
　　155 x 195 cm/62 x 78 in

Backing
155 x 195 cm/62 x 78 in

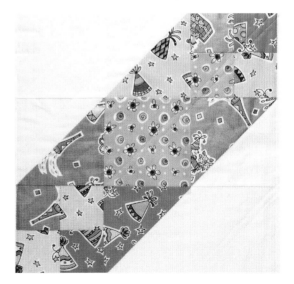

CUTTING

1 From the white fabric, cut 12 strips, 11.5 cm/4½ in deep, across the width of the fabric. Cross-cut to produce 31 rectangles, 11.5 x 31.5 cm/4½ x 12½ in, and 24 squares each 11.5 cm/4½ in. Cut three strips, 12.5 cm/4⅞ in deep, across the width of the fabric. Cross-cut into 24 squares each 12.5 cm/4⅞ in.

2 From the print fabrics, cut 12 strips, 6.5 cm/2½ in deep, across the width of fabric for the four-patch units.

3 Cut 4 strips, 12.5 cm/4⅞ in deep, across the width of the fabric and cross-cut to produce 24 squares, 12.5 cm/4⅞ in. Trim the remaining strips to 11.5 cm/4½ in deep and cross-cut to produce 12 squares, 11.5 cm/4½ in.

4 From the border fabric, cut six strips, 6.5 cm/2½ in deep, across the width of the fabric.

5 From the binding fabric, cut eight strips, 6.5 cm/2½ in deep, across the width of the fabric.

STITCHING

1 Stitch the 6.5 cm/2½ in wide print strips together in pairs of different colours, right sides together, down one long edge, taking an accurate 7.5 mm/¼ in seam allowance.

Press flat on the stitching line to relax the stitching, then press the seam towards the darker fabric.

2 Cross-cut the pieced strips at 6.5 cm/ 2½ in intervals to produce 88 two-patch units (diagram 1).

DIAGRAM 1

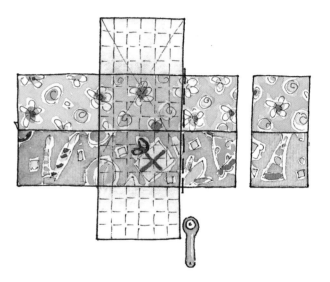

3 Chain-stitch random pairs together to produce 44 four-patch units for the blocks and the sashing posts (diagram 2). Press.

DIAGRAM 2

5 Cut along the marked line. Press towards the print fabric and trim the corners. The resulting half-square triangles should measure 11.5 cm/4½ in. Repeat to make 48 half-square triangles.

6 Set out the four-patch units, half-square triangles and plain squares in the block pattern (diagram 4). Stitch the blocks together first in rows, then stitch the rows together to form the block.

DIAGRAM 4

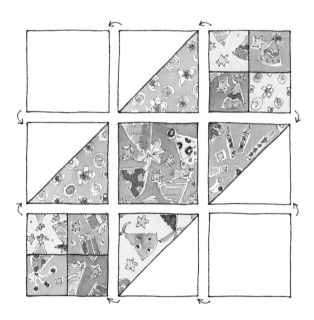

4 On the white 12.5 cm/4⅞ in squares mark the diagonal in pencil on the wrong side of the fabric. Place a white 12.5 cm/4⅞ in square on a print 12.5 cm/4⅞ in square, right sides together, and stitch 7.5 mm/¼ in away on each side of the marked line (diagram 3).

DIAGRAM 3

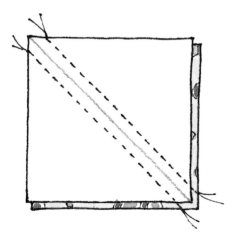

7 Following the quilt assembly diagram, stitch four rows of three blocks together with a white 11.5 x 31.5 cm/4½ x 12½ in sashing strip at the beginning and end, and between each block.

8 Stitch five rows of sashing strips and sashing posts together, three strips and four posts in each row, beginning and ending with a post.

9 Join the rows of blocks and sashing to complete the pieced top.

10 Join the six border strips into one long length. Measure the pieced top through the centre from top to bottom, then cut two border strips to this measurement. Stitch to the sides of the quilt. Press seams towards the borders.

11 Measure the pieced top through the centre from side to side, then cut two more border strips to this measurement. Stitch to the top and bottom. Press seams towards the borders.

NOTE Check that the stitching lines are an accurate 1.5 cm/½ in apart before cutting between them.

FINISHING

1 Spread the backing right side down on a flat surface, then smooth out the wadding and the patchwork top, right side up, on top. Fasten together with safety pins or baste in a grid.

2 Quilt in-the-ditch vertically and horizontally along the sashing. Quilt the blocks 7.5 mm/¼ in away from the diagonal seams. Trim the excess wadding and backing level with the pieced top.

3 Join the binding strips with diagonal seams to make a continuous length to fit all round the quilt and use to bind the edges with a double-fold binding, mitred at the corners.

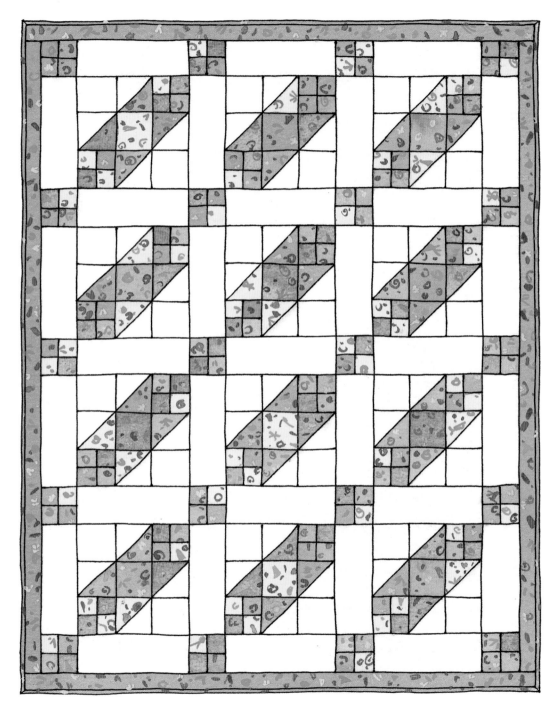

Blue-and-white Ohio Stars Bed Quilt

A galaxy of blue stars sparkle on this single bed quilt, which is edged with a "Folded Ribbon" border. A quick method used for the Ohio Stars helps to achieve accurate star points. A selection of blue fabrics has been used against a unifying white-on-white floral sprig for the background.

NOTE For the binding, use the same fabric as the background so that it does not detract attention from the star blocks and ribbon border. If you do the same, you will not need any extra binding fabric as you can cut the binding from the amount allowed for the plain borders.

Finished size
178 x 224 cm/70 in x 88 in

Materials
All fabrics used are 100 per cent cotton.

For the background and borders
    White-on-white floral sprig: 6.1 m/
    6¼ yd (ask for this in two pieces
    3.85 m/3¾ yd for the star backgrounds
    and 2.25 m/2½ yd for the borders and
    binding)

Binding
    20 in/50 cm (if a different colour from
    background fabric is used, see the
    note above)

For the stars
    Various small floral blue prints:
    1.75 m/2 yd or equivalent in scraps (as
    a rough guide, a metric fat quarter will
    yield eight stars, and you will need a
    total of 48 stars)

For the folded ribbon border
    Dark blue, 25 cm/10 in; medium blue,
    90 cm/1 yd

Backing
    4.75 m/5 yd

Wadding
    188 x 233 cm/74 x 92 in

NOTE Cutting from the length of the fabric avoids joins. There is also less stretch in the fabric, which is helpful when attaching long, narrow borders such as these, especially when stitching to a bias edge.

CUTTING

1 From the 2.25 m/2½ yd piece of white fabric, cut eight strips, 9 cm/3½ in wide, down the length of the fabric for the borders. These will be trimmed to fit. Cut four 6 cm/2½ in strips, also from the length of the fabric, for the binding. (If you are using a different-coloured binding, cut eight 6 cm/2½ in strips from the width of the binding fabric.)

2 From the remaining piece of white fabric, cut 10 strips, 11 cm/4¼ in deep, across the width and cross-cut these into 96 squares for the star points. Cut 16 strips, 9 cm/3½ in deep, across the width and cross-cut into 192 squares for the corners of the star blocks. Cut six strips, 9 cm/3½ in deep, across the width for the folded ribbon border. Cut two squares each 11 cm/4¼ in and cut these in half diagonally for the four corner triangles.

3 From each of the fabrics chosen for the stars, cut strips, 11 cm/4¼ in deep, across the width of the fabric and cross-cut these into squares. You will need a total of 96 squares for the star points. Cut 48 squares each 9 cm/3½ in for the star centres.

4 From the dark blue ribbon border fabric, cut three strips, 6 cm/2½ in deep, across the width.

5 From the medium blue ribbon border fabric, cut ten strips, 6 cm/2½ in deep, across the width and cross-cut nine of these strips into 44 lengths each 20 cm/8 in (each strip will yield five, so you will have one extra length), plus four 25.5 cm/10 in lengths from the remaining strip for the corners.

STITCHING

1 Draw a diagonal line with a pencil across the wrong side of each of the 96 white 11 cm/4¼ in squares, which will form the background to the star points.

2 Take one blue 11 cm/4¼ in square and place it right sides together with one of the white squares you have just marked. Stitch a seam line 7.5 mm/¼ in away on each side of the drawn line (diagram 1). Repeat with the remaining 95 pairs of squares. Chain piecing will save time and thread.

DIAGRAM 1

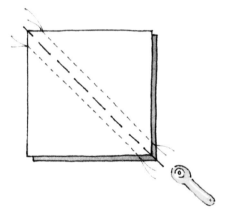

3 Cut the threads between the squares. Press each stitched pair of squares flat to set the seams, then cut along the drawn diagonal line. Press the seams towards the darker fabric.

4 Take half of the units and, on the wrong side, draw a diagonal line in the opposite direction from the seam. Take one unmarked unit and put it right sides together with a marked unit, so that the white half of one unit is on top of the blue half of the other and vice versa. Stitch a 7.5 mm/¼ in seam on each side of the drawn diagonal (diagram 2).

DIAGRAM 2

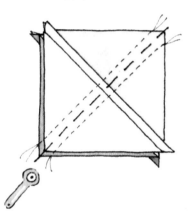

5 Repeat with all the remaining pairs of half square units, then press each pair flat to set the seams before cutting along the drawn diagonal line.

6 Press each stitched unit open. You should have 192 quarter-square units, four for each star block in the quilt, and each should measure 9 cm/3½ in. Trim off the "ears".

7 Stitch two quarter square units to one matching blue 9 cm/3½ in square and stitch two white background 9 cm/3½ in squares to each side of two more quarter square units as shown in diagram 3. Press seam allowances towards the whole squares.

8 Join the three rows of units together to make one star block (diagram 3). Press the seam allowances towards the centre square. Repeat to make a total of 48 star blocks.

DIAGRAM 3

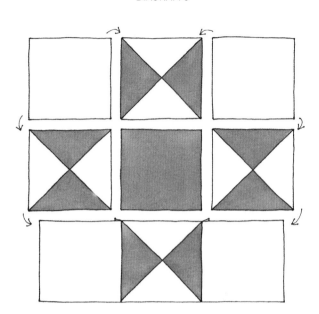

9 When all the blocks have been pieced, stitch the blocks together into eight rows of six blocks as shown in the quilt assembly plan. Press the seams between the blocks in opposite directions for alternate rows.

10 When all the rows have been joined, press the top lightly.

ADDING THE BORDERS

1 To add the inner plain white borders, measure the pieced top through the centre from top to bottom and trim two of the white 9 cm/3½ in border strips to this length. Pin and stitch to the sides of the pieced top. Press the seam allowances towards the borders. Measure the pieced top through the centre from side to side, then trim two more strips to this measurement. Stitch to the top and bottom and press as before.

2 To make the folded ribbon border, stitch one dark blue 6 cm/2½ in wide strip between two white background 9 cm/ 3½ in strips along the long sides, taking a 7.5 mm/¼ in seam allowance and being careful not to stretch and curve the strips as you are sewing. Repeat with the remaining two dark blue strips and four white strips. Press the seam allowances towards the dark blue fabric.

3 Cross-cut the three strip sets into 46 rectangles, 6 cm/2½ in wide (diagram 4).

DIAGRAM 4

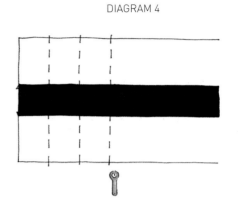

4 Stitch one of these rectangles to one medium blue 6 x 20 cm/2½ x 8 in rectangle as follows: mark a crease halfway down the white top part of the rectangle and line up the top of the medium blue strip with this crease mark, right sides together (diagram 5).

DIAGRAM 5

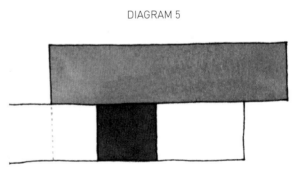

5 Stitch together. Stitch the remaining rectangles together in pairs with half of the medium blue strips to the right-hand edge of the slice, and half to the left-hand edge. You will have 22 of each and two spare slices. Press towards the medium blue strip.

6 Stitch six of the left-handed units together in a staggered row, lining up the bottom of the medium blue strip so that it is 7.5 mm/¼ in beyond the bottom of the adjoining dark blue square (diagram 6a). Press the seams towards the medium blue strips. Repeat with six of the right-handed units (6b).

DIAGRAM 6A (LEFT) AND 6B (RIGHT)

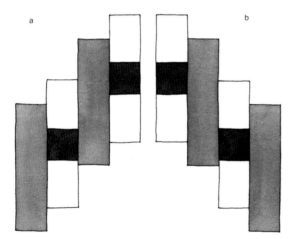

7 Trim away the ends of the strips in a straight line, taking care to ensure that there is a 7.5 mm/¼ in seam allowance beyond the points of the dark blue squares (diagram 7).

DIAGRAM 7

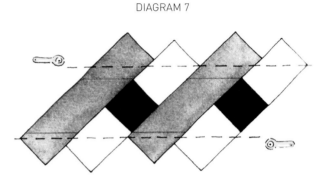

8 Study the quilt assembly plan and you will see that there are two different ways of reversing the direction of the folded ribbon, so as to keep the corners of the quilt the same. Depending on the size of your patchwork top, you may find that one or the other method will help your border fit better. Instructions for both methods follow.

9 Pin the border strips along one side of the patchwork top, starting at each end and handling the strips with care, as these are now all cut bias edges. Decide on the most suitable method of joining the strips at the mid-point. If your medium blue strips are close enough to overlap (as at the top and bottom of this quilt), piece in a small background triangle cut to fit the space available.

10 If your medium-blue strips only just meet, however (as at the sides of this quilt), take one of the spare rectangles and unpick the top background piece, joining it onto the other side of the dark blue square so that the unit can be trimmed into a triangle to fit the space available (diagram 8). Whichever treatment is chosen, you must use the same method on the opposite border, although you can use different methods for the sides and top and bottom, as in the quilt photographed.

DIAGRAM 8

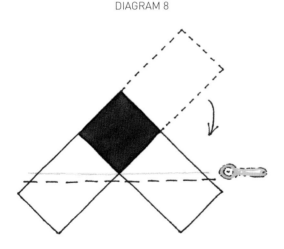

NOTE If you find you are having difficulty making the folded ribbon border fit, you may be able to reduce the width of the inner plain border, or add a narrow "filler" strip, to bring the top up to the size you need.

11 Now join the strip units to make the other side border, using six right-handed and six left-handed units, and press and trim as before. When stitching the border strips to the quilt, check the quilt assembly diagram to make sure that the ribbon is going in the right direction, leaving the corners open for the longer strips to be added last. Press the seam allowances towards the inner plain border.

12 Join the remaining strip units and attach them to the top and bottom. This time, there will only be five right-handed and five left-handed units for each.

13 Take the four 25.5 cm/10 in medium blue strips and stitch them diagonally across the corners to complete the ribbon. Press the seam allowance towards the ribbon and trim to square off the corners. Add the white corner triangles and press the seam allowance towards the ribbon.

14 Finally, attach the outer plain borders to the sides first and then to the top and bottom, measuring through the middle of the quilt as before, and taking particular care when stitching them in place that you do not stretch the bias edges of the folded ribbon border. Press towards the outer edges of the quilt top.

FINISHING

1 Measure the completed quilt top and cut and piece the backing to fit with at least 5 cm/2 in all round. If you are joining the backing, don't forget to cut off the selvages as these are very tightly woven and can cause distortion in the quilt. Press the seam open.

2 Spread the backing right side down on a flat surface, then smooth out the wadding and the patchwork top, right side up, on top. Fasten together with safety pins or baste in a grid.

3 Mark the top with the desired quilting design. Quilt in-the-ditch along the seam lines between the blocks, then add additional straight lines by quilting in-the-ditch along the seams on each side of the star centres. Quilt long diagonal lines in-the-ditch through the star point units:

the continuation of the diagonal lines forms a secondary square on point quilting pattern between the stars. These diagonals were marked with a plastic tool called a Hera marker and a long ruler; the marker makes an indentation in the layered quilt that shows up well on light-coloured fabric. Finally, quilt the plain borders 7.5 mm/¼ in in from the seam lines.

4 Join the binding strips with diagonal seams to make a continuous length to fit all round the quilt and use to bind the edges with a double-fold binding, mitred at the corners.

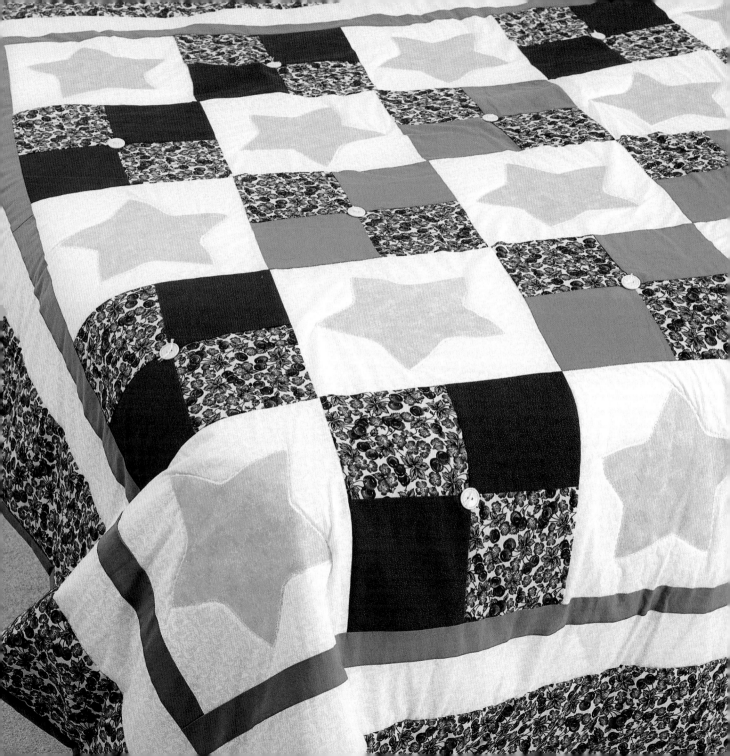

Summer Fields

The fresh pink, green and white fabrics reminiscent of strawberries and the curvy star shape of buttercups in the fields in summertime. The quilt is simply pieced with four-patch blocks and alternating plain squares with an appliquéed star.

Finished size
183 x 183 cm/73 x 73 in

Materials
All fabrics used are 100 per cent cotton.

For the Four-patch Blocks and
Outer Border
    Pink and green patterned fabric:
    3 m/3 yd

For the four-patch blocks
    Pink: 50 cm/20in

For the Four-patch Blocks, Inner Border
and Binding
    Green: 1.1 m/1¼ yd

For the Alternate Blocks and Middle Border
    White: 3 m/3 yd

For the stars
    Yellow: 50 cm/20 in

Backing
4 m/4¼ yd

Fusible web
    75 cm/30 in

Wadding
    193 x 193 cm/77 x 77 in

12 buttons

CUTTING

1 From the pink and green patterned fabric, cut three strips, 14 cm/5½ in deep, across the width of the fabric. Cut four strips, 16.5 cm/6½ in wide, from the length for the outer border.

2 From the pink fabric, cut two strips, 14 cm/5½ in deep, across the width of the fabric.

3 From the green fabric, cut one strip, 14 cm/5½ in deep, across the width of the fabric. Cut six strips, 7.5 cm/3 in deep, across the width for the binding. Cut six strips, 5 cm/2 in deep, across the width for the inner border.

4 From the white fabric, cut 13 squares each 26.5 cm/10½ in. Cut four strips, 9 cm/3½ in wide, from the length for the middle border.

5 Using the template plastic, enlarge and make a star template from the template provided.

6 Cut the backing fabric in half crosswise.

STITCHING

1 Place one patterned and one pink 14 cm/5½ in strip right sides together and stitch along one long side, taking a 7.5 mm/¼ in seam (diagram 1). Press towards the darker fabric. Repeat with the remaining two patterned and pink strips.

DIAGRAM 1

2 Place one patterned and one green 14 cm/5½ in strip right sides together and stitch along one long side, taking a 7.5 mm/¼ in seam. Press towards the darker fabric.

3 Trim the selvages from all of the strips, then sub-cut into 14 cm/5½ in sections. Reversing the colour sequence, stitch two pairs of these sections together to make four-patch squares (diagram 2). You will need a total of eight pink-and-patterned squares and four green-and-patterned squares.

4 Iron fusible web onto the wrong side of the yellow fabric, then using the template provided, trace the star shape onto the backing paper 13 times. Cut out the stars. Peel off the paper backing and position the stars in the middle of each of the white 26.5 cm/10½ in squares. Iron in place following the instructions on the fusible web for the heat setting.

TEMPLATE

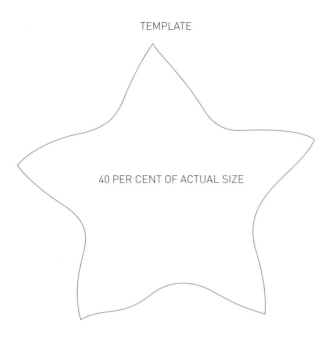

40 PER CENT OF ACTUAL SIZE

DIAGRAM 2

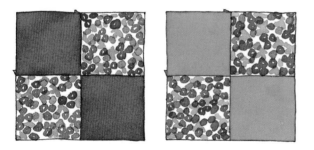

5 Using a decorative stitch, stitch all around each star, starting on a long side (not a point). Stitch a small section at a time. When reaching a point of the star, leave the needle in the down position and lift the machine foot and pivot the work slightly to re-align it to stitch the next section. When the whole star has been

sewn, run over a few stitches to lock the thread, drawing the ends through to the back of the work and secure.

6 Following the quilt assembly diagram, arrange the four-patch squares and star squares in five rows of five squares. Mark each row on the back of a white square lightly in pencil to keep the rows in sequence.

7 Stitch the squares in each row together and press the seams towards the darker squares. Then stitch the rows together, pressing the seams all in the same direction.

ADDING THE BORDERS

1 To add the inner border, cut two of the 5 cm/2 in green strips in half and stitch one to each of the remaining four green strips. Measure the pieced top through the centre from top to bottom, then trim two of the strips to this measurement. Stitch to the sides of the quilt. Press towards the border. Measure the pieced top through the centre from side to side, then trim the remaining two strips to this measurement. Pin and stitch to the top and bottom and press as before.

2 To add the middle border, measure the pieced top through the centre from top to bottom, then trim two of the strips to this measurement. Stitch to the sides of the quilt. Press towards the inner border. Measure the pieced top through the centre from side to side, then trim the remaining two strips to this measurement. Pin and stitch to the top and bottom and press as before.

3 To add the outer border, measure the pieced top through the centre from top to bottom, then trim two of the strips to this measurement. Stitch to the sides of the quilt. Press towards the outer border. Measure the pieced top through the centre from side to side, then trim the remaining two strips to this measurement. Pin and stitch to the top and bottom and press as before.

4 To make the backing, place the two rectangles right sides together and stitch down the longer side. Press the seam to one side, then trim to make a square, 193 cm/77 in.

5 Spread the backing right side down on a flat surface, then smooth out the wadding and the patchwork top, right side up, on top. Fasten together with safety pins or baste in a grid.

6 Machine quilt round the stars, then using white embroidery thread, stitch buttons in the middle of each four-patch square, leaving a length of thread to tie in the centre of the button. Trim to the length required (diagram 3).

DIAGRAM 3

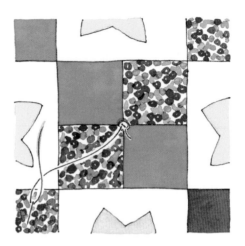

7 Stitch the eight 7.5 cm/3 in green binding strips together in pairs to make four long strips. Fold the strips in half lengthwise, right sides together, and press. Place one strip along one side of the quilt, aligning the raw edges, trim to fit and stitch taking the usual seam allowance. Fold to the back of the quilt and hem stitch in place along the stitching line. Repeat on the opposite side.

8 For the remaining two sides, stitch the strips to the quilt in the same way, but before folding to the back trim the strips so that they are 7.5 mm/¼ in longer than the quilt at each end. Fold in the short overlap, then fold the binding to the back and hem stitch in place.

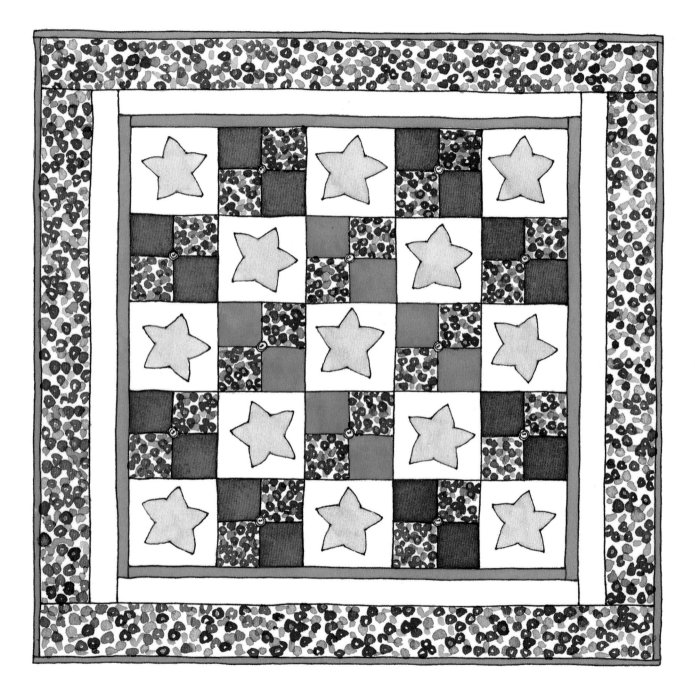

Floral Garland Quilt

Combine five dainty floral prints with a white-on-white fabric for a delicate quilt to decorate a summer bedroom. The illusion that the blocks are floating is achieved by using the same fabric in the block backgrounds as for the alternate setting blocks and borders.

Finished size
204 x 167 cm/87 x 73 in

Materials
All fabrics used are 100 per cent cotton.

White
    5 m/5½ yd

Floral prints
    Five soft pastel floral prints: 30 cm/
    12 in of each

Wadding
    219 x 182 cm/93 x 79 in

Backing cotton
    219 x 182 cm/93 x 79 in

Binding
    90 cm/1 yd extra of one of the
    floral fabrics

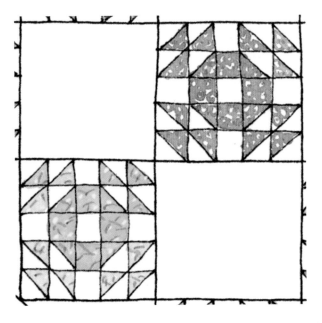

CUTTING

The white fabric for the borders, edge and corner triangles and squares is cut at this stage. The remaining fabrics are cut as the blocks are stitched.

1 From the white fabric, cut four strips, 22 x 189 cm/8½ x 74 in, down the length of the fabric for the borders.

2 Cut three squares, 40 cm/15¾ in; cross-cut these across both diagonals to make 12 side triangles. Use one of these as a template to cut two more triangles to make a total of 14 triangles.

3 Cut two 20.5 cm/8 in squares; cut these across one diagonal to make four corner triangles.

4 Cut 12 squares each 26.5 cm/10½ in for the alternate setting blocks.

STITCHING

Make the blocks four at a time using one of the floral prints combined with the white for each set of four.

1 Cutting across the width of the fabric, cut three strips, 7.5 cm/2⅞ in deep, and one strip, 6.5 cm/2½ in deep, from one of the floral fabrics and the same from the white fabric.

2 Place one floral and one white 7.5 cm/2⅞ in strip right sides together. On the wrong side of the white strip, mark off 7.5 cm/2⅞ in squares, then draw a continuous zigzag line from corner to corner of the marked squares along the length of the strip. Stitch both sides of this line 7.5 mm/¼ in away. This can be done in a continuous line, using a 7.5 mm/¼ in foot on your sewing machine. If you do not have this facility, mark the sewing line before stitching (diagram 1).

DIAGRAM 1

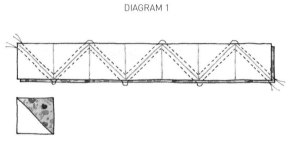

3 Cut on the vertical and diagonal lines. Repeat with the second set of strips (one floral and one white), then cut a 30.5 cm/ 12 in section from each of the remaining two 7.5 cm/2⅞ in strips and mark out four more squares. Stitch and cut as before. Press the resulting triangle units open (64 altogether).

4 Take what remains of the third set of 7.5 cm/2⅞ in strips and cut the width down to 6.5 cm/2½ in. Cut a 53.5 cm/21 in length from both the floral and the white strips. Stitch these together along one long side. Press the seam, then cross-cut into eight 6.5 cm/2½ in segments to make the shorter square units (diagram 2).

DIAGRAM 2

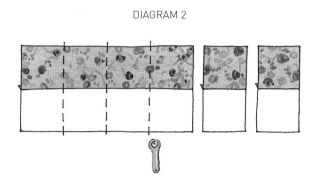

DIAGRAM 3

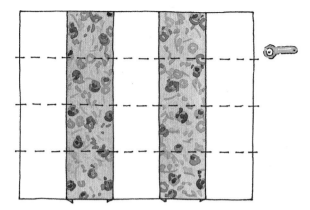

5 To make the longer square units, cut three 28 cm/11 in long strips, 6.5 cm/ 2½ in deep, from the remaining white strip and two 28 cm/11 in long strips from the remaining floral strip. Stitch these strips together along the long sides, taking the usual seam allowance, in the sequence: white/floral/white/floral/white. Press the seams towards the darker fabric, then cross cut into four 6.5 cm/2½ in segments (diagram 3).

6 Using four of the triangle units made in step 3, make four corner sections for each block, 16 altogether (diagram 4).

DIAGRAM 4

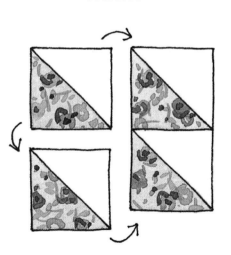

7 To complete the blocks, arrange the block sections in the correct order as shown in diagram 5 and stitch together.

DIAGRAM 6

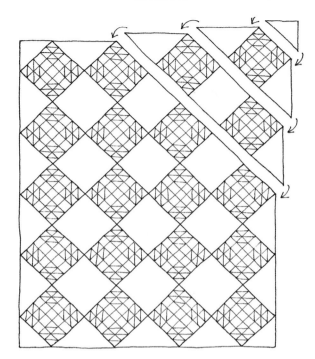

DIAGRAM 5

8 Repeat this process with the remaining four floral fabrics to make 20 blocks.

9 Press the pieced blocks thoroughly and, if necessary, adjust the size of the alternate blocks to fit the pieced blocks.

10 Following diagram 6, arrange and stitch the pieced blocks alternately with the plain squares in diagonal rows, adding the corner and side triangles as you work.

11 Press the seams, then stitch the rows together, matching the seams as you work.

ADDING THE BORDERS

1 Measure the pieced top through the centre from top to bottom, then trim two of the white border strips to this measurement. Stitch to the sides of the quilt.

2 Measure the pieced top through the centre from side to side, then trim the remaining two white border strips to this measurement. Stitch to the top and bottom.

FINISHING

1 If you plan to do your own quilting, spread the backing right side down on a flat surface, then smooth the wadding and the quilt top, right sides up on top. Fasten together with safety pins or baste in a grid.

2 Using the free motion quilting method, quilt over the surface of the quilt in machine quilting thread.

3 Using the extra floral fabric, cut eight strips, 9 cm/3½ in deep, for the binding.

4 Join the binding strips with diagonal seams to make a continuous length to fit all round the quilt and use to bind the edges with a double-fold binding, mitred at the corners.

Index

Backing and binding fabrics 10
Blue-and-white Ohio Stars Bed Quilt 106
Borders 23
Chain-piecing 21
Diamond Quilt 54
Fan Quilt 42
Floral Garland Quilt 122
Half-square triangles 21
Hidden Stars 75
Jacob's Ladder 100
Layer cake 37
Long-arm quilting machines 12
Patchwork fabrics 10
    Preparation 11
Portugal Strippy 32
Pressing 23
Quarter-square triangles 22
Quillow 48
Quilting 24
    Hand quilting 27
    Machine quilting 26
Rotary cutting 13, 15
    Cross-cutting 17
    Cutting strips 16

Making the edge straight 15
    Seams 19
    Triangles 18
Row of Flowers 83
Sewing machines 12
    Quick machine piecing 21
Sister's Choice 88
Spider's Web 94
Squares and Stars 67
Summer Fields 116
Twinkling Star 60
Threads 12
Useful Equipment 14
    Binding 29
    Hoops and frames 15
    Markers 14
    Needles 14
    Pins 14
    Safety pins 14
    Scissors 14
    Thimbles 14
Wadding (batting) 11
    Quantities 11
Water's Edge 36